Prepare for the
Great Tribulation
and the Era of Peace

Volume LXXIII
(Volume 73)

October 1, 2013 – December 31, 2013

by

John Leary

Queenship
PUBLISHING COMPANY
P.O. Box 220 • Goleta, CA 93116
(800) 647-9882 • (805) 692-0043 • Fax: (805) 967-5133
www.queenship.org

Dedication

To the Most Holy Trinity

God

The Father, Son and Holy Spirit

The Source of

All

Life, Love and Wisdom

Cover art by Josyp Terelya

Library of Congress Number # 95-73237

Published by:
    Queenship Publishing
    P.O. Box 220
    Goleta, CA 93116
(800) 647-9882 • (805) 692-0043 • Fax: (805) 967-5133
    www.queenship.org

Printed in the United States of America

ISBN: 978-1-57918-430-8

Acknowledgments

It is in a spirit of deep gratitude that I would like to acknowledge first the Holy Trinity: Father, (Jesus), and the Holy Spirit; the Blessed Virgin Mary and the many saints and angels who have made this book possible.

My wife, Carol, has been an invaluable partner. Her complete support of faith and prayers has allowed us to work as a team. This was especially true in the many hours of indexing and proofing of the manuscript. All of our family have been a source of care and support.

I am greatly indebted to Josyp Terelya for his very gracious offer to provide the art work for this publication. He has spent three months of work and prayer to provide us with a selection of many original pictures. He wanted very much to enhance the visions and messages with these beautiful and provocative works. You will experience some of them throughout these volumes.

A very special thank you goes to my spiritual director, Fr. Leo J. Klem, C.S.B. No matter what hour I called him, he was always there with his confident wisdom, guidance and discernment. His love, humility, deep faith and trust are a true inspiration.

Equal gratitude also goes to our prior spiritual advisor, Father Donald McCarthy, C.S.B.

My appreciation also goes to Father John V. Rosse, my good pastor who is retiring from Holy Name of Jesus Church. He has been open, loving and supportive from the very beginning.

There are many friends and relatives whose interest, love and prayerful support have been a real gift from God. Our own Wednesday, Monday and First Saturday prayer groups deserve a special thank you for their loyalty and faithfulness.

Finally, I would like to thank Bob and Claire Schaefer of Queenship Publishing for providing the opportunity to bring this message of preparation, love and warnings to you, the people of God.

John Leary, Jr.

Declaration

The decree of the Congregation for the Propagation of the Faith, A.A.S.58, 1186 (approved by Pope Paul VI on October 14, 1966), states that the Nihil Obstat and Imprimatur are no longer required on publications that deal with private revelations, provided they contain nothing contrary to faith and morals.

The author wishes to manifest unconditional submission to the final and official judgement of the Magisterium of the Church.

His Holiness, Pope Urban VII states:

In cases which concern private revelations, it is better to believe than to not believe, for if you believe, and it is proven true, you will be happy that you have believed, because our Holy Mother asked it. If you believe, and it should be proven false, you will receive all blessings as if it had been true, because you believed it to be true. (Pope Urban III, 1623-44)

The Catechism of the Catholic Church states:

Pg. 23, #67: Throughout the ages, there have been so-called 'private revelations,' some of which have been recognized by the authority of the Church. They do not belong, however, to the deposit of faith. It is not their role to improve or complete Christ's definitive Revelation, but to help live more fully by it in a certain period of history. Guided by the Magisterium of the Church, the sensus fidelium knows how to discern and welcome in these revelations whatever constitutes an authentic call of Christ or His saints to the Church.

Publisher's Foreword

John has, with some exceptions, reported receiving messages twice a day since they began in July, 1993. The first of the day usually takes place during morning Mass, immediately after he receives the Eucharist. If the name of the church is not mentioned, it is a local Rochester, NY church. When out of town, the church name is included in the text. The second occurs in the evening, either at Perpetual Adoration or at the prayer group that is held at Holy Name of Jesus Church.

Various names appear in the text. Most of the time, the names appear only once or twice. Their identity is not important to the message and their reason for being in the text is evident. First names have been used, when requested by the individual.

We are grateful to Josyp Terelya for the cover art, as well as for the art throughout the book. Josyp is a well-known visionary and also the author of *Witness* and most recently *In the Kingdom of the Spirit*.

Early in 1999 John's bishop established a special commission to read John's published works and to talk to him about his religious experiences. The commission rendered its report in June. By letter of June 25, 1999 John was advised to have an explanatory note printed in the front of each book. This note appears on page ix of this edition. The first edition under these rules resulted in a delay of 90 days.

As of January 2013, John has a new spiritual director, Rev. Joseph A. Grasso, C.PP.S.

Fr. Frederick W. Bush continues to review the messages.

Previously the messages were being reviewed by Rev. Donald McCarthy, C.S.B., who was John's spiritual advisor. He has retired due to medical reasons.

Late in October, 1999 John Leary and Carol were called to the office of the Diocese of Rochester for a meeting with the Vicar General. The result of the meeting was that they (the Diocese) are now allowing John to publish under their obedience. John was cautioned against mentioning the subjects called to John's attention in the bishop's original declaration (see page ix). John was further ordered to have his spiritual advisor read and approve each book which is being done.

This volume covers messages from October 1, 2013 through December 31, 2013. The volumes have been coming out quarterly due to the urgency of the messages.

The Publisher

Readers Please Note:

Bishop Matthew H. Clark, Bishop of Rochester, has accepted the unanimous judgment of a special mixed Commission set up to study the writings of John Leary. After reading the volumes and meeting with Mr. Leary, they testified that they found him psychologically sound and spiritually serious. They concluded that his locutions are not a fraud perpetrated on the Catholic community. Nevertheless, in their judgment, his locutions are of human origin, the normal workings of the mind in the process of mental prayer.

Of grave concern to the Bishop and the Commission, however, are the errors that have found their way into his writings, two of which are most serious. The first is called by the Church millenarianism. This erroneous teaching, contained in the first 6 volumes of *Prepare for the Great Tribulation and the Era of Peace,* holds that Christ will return to reign on the earth for a thousand years at the end of time. As the *Catechism of the Catholic Church* expresses it:

> The Antichrist's deception already begins to take shape in the world every time the claim is made to realize within history that messianic hope which can only be realized beyond history through the eschatological judgment. The Church has rejected even modified forms of this falsification of the kingdom to come under the name millenarianism ... (CCC #676).

The second error is anti-papalism. While the Church holds that the Pope by reason of his office as Vicar of Christ, namely, as pastor of the entire Church, has full, supreme and universal power over the whole Church (Vatican II, Constitution on the Church, #22), Mr. Leary's locutions select Pope John Paul II to be obeyed but his successor to be ignored as an imposter pope. This erroneous teaching is found in all the volumes.

Because Mr. Leary has reaffirmed the teaching and discipline of the Church and acknowledged the teaching authority of John Paul II and Bishop Matthew H. Clark and their successors, Bishop Clark has permitted these volumes to be published with this warning to its readers appended.

Visions and Messages
of John Leary:

Tuesday, October 1, 2013: (St. Therese of Lisieux)

At Holy Name after Communion, I could see St. Therese come to greet me as one of my spiritual directors. St. Therese said: *"My people, I thank you for listening to my words of advice, as I am always directing you to the love of my Jesus. You are familiar with my 'Little Way' in my writings, and how I treated every little task as an opportunity to do something for the love of my Jesus. You read about my writings many years ago, so maybe it would benefit you now to re-read them. You have grown in your faith to understand where I was being led, so reading my words could help you more. The more you want to help Jesus, the more you want to reach out to people in love, even in loving those people, who you do not like. Jesus asked us to love everyone, and this is one of your earthly challenges that you should take to heart in your striving for perfection. You know how I suffered from my sickness at the end of my life. Now, you need to offer up all that you do to Jesus out of love for Him."*

Later, at St. Theodore's Adoration, I could see baby arms and legs floating down a sewer, and in garbage dumps. Jesus said: *"My people of America, what are you doing in murdering My babies and disposing of them down the sewer and in garbage dumps? Have you no fear of My punishment for your brutal sins against these children? I have warned Americans before that if you do not restrict your abortions, then I will do it in a way that you do not want to know. Killing My babies is causing Me to suffer greatly, and your nation will pay dearly for your grisly killings. Your society has become so evil that each new sin will put another nail in your coffin. Many of your states allow same sex marriage which glorifies homosexual acts that are abominations of sin in My eyes. Other states also allow euthanasia which will be promoted more by your Obamacare Law when they stop treating older patients for needed operations. Also, in your Obamacare Law there is a plan to mandate the mark of the beast or a computer chip in the body that will control your mind and make you into a robot. Refuse to take any chip in the body, even if the authorities threaten to kill you. With all of these evils being flaunted by your government authorities, your country will suffer much for your sins. It is just a matter of time when your rights will be taken away, as the one world people will take you over with a planned martial law. My faithful need to be prepared to leave for My refuges, when I warn you to go, as your lives and souls will be in danger. Your country's days are numbered, before My judgment and your punishment will come upon you."*

Wednesday, October 2, 2013: (Guardian Angel Day)

At St. John the Evangelist after Communion, I saw Mark, my guardian angel, with a light leading my way. Mark, my guardian angel, said: *"I am Mark, and I stand before God, as I was commanded to watch over you. I want you to be more observant of how I am here to guide you in physical and spiritual ways. When you are looking for direction, or you need some help, you can call on Me through Jesus to help you. When you have a sense of a good intention, it is me prodding you to do the right thing. The more you are in sin, the harder it is to hear me helping you, so keep coming to Confession at least monthly. We are not allowed to interfere with your free will, but learn from your mistakes to do things better out of love for God. We angels have a better understanding of God's Divine Will, and we are trying to guide you on the right path to heaven, and following God's Will."*

Later, at St. Theodore's Adoration, I could see a spider spinning its web. Jesus said: *"My people, this vision of a spider on its web is a sign of your internet world wide web. This communication has allowed e-mail to send messages, data, and even movies over this line. It is used by businesses to sell things, and for web sites to post information that is searched by search engines. In your quest for information, there are various organizations that track what you search for, in order to sell you things with copious e-mail ads and even pop-ups. You also see that some people put viruses on the internet to shut you down, or use your computer to send ads. Even your government spy groups watch all of your communications supposedly to catch terrorists or crooks. Your e-mails can be used against you as evidence in trials. Beware of using this system that can be used against you. The evil ones will take over, and control the internet, so the Antichrist will be able to post his picture and commands to seduce you into worshiping him. After the Warning, you need to get rid of all of your electronic devices that are connected to the internet. It is by these devices that these evil ones could track your movements. Without any chips on you, it would be hard to find you. I will also place an invisible shield around you, so they could not even track the chip in your car's ignition system."*

Thursday, October 3, 2013:

At Holy Name after Communion, I could see Jesus preparing His disciples to go out and evangelize souls. Jesus said: *"My people, in today's Gospel I am sending out My disciples to spread the news of how the Kingdom of God is at hand. I am also inviting all of My faithful to come to Me so they can have a true love relationship with Me. You receive Me in Holy Communion, and I am intimately sharing My love with you. If you truly love Me, then you will love Me in your neighbor as well. The greatest sharing in My love, is to share your faith with others, in inviting them to have a close personal love relationship with Me, as you have. The best gift that you could give someone, is a gift of faith in Me for saving their soul from hell. All of My faithful are promised to be with Me eventually in heaven forever. Sharing this promise with new believers is the most important moment of their lives, when they find Me in their own hearts. Ask people to open the doors to their hearts, so I can come in and dwell with them. The joy of these souls in accepting Me, is magnified in heaven for every soul that repents and is converted to the faith."*

Later, at the Eternal Father prayer group at Holy Name Adoration, I could see a major gridlock over Obamacare in the shutdown and later on the Debt Ceiling. Jesus said: *"My people, it is dramatic to shut down the government over Obamacare, but many Republicans are making a stand over an unfair law that forces people to buy health insurance or pay a penalty. This alone is against your freedoms. It is difficult for some who could not afford health insurance, but now people will be forced to pay for everyone's health at a higher price. Finding enough doctors will be another problem. The worst of this law is that people will be forced to pay for abortion, and they will be forced to take chips in the body. All the taxes from this law could ruin your economy by making larger deficits than you have now. Pray that some compromise on this Health Law can be found to limit the damage of a shutdown and a possible default."*

I could see two more legislative issues that could be pushed through without the consent of all the people. Jesus said: *"My people, you have seen the courts force abortion and Obamacare on you. The next two abominations will be same sex marriage and euthanasia which the same Godless people will be forcing through your evil courts. If these evil ones cannot get enough votes to pass such evil laws, then they go through the back door in your evil court system. When you legalize killing and same sex marriage, you are doing so against My Commandments. You wonder why I am bringing My punishment against you, but look at the blood on your hands, and you have the answer."*

I could see a time when people lived a slower paced life, and without electricity. Jesus said: *"My people, you have been living a very comfortable lifestyle as you have been spoiled by your many electrical devices. Unfortunately, you are spending less time in prayer with Me* because of these distractions. *When you come to live at My refuges, My angels will be protecting you, but you may see little use of any electricity. This will be a more rustic life, but you will have more time for prayer, and you will be healed of your ailments. Trust in Me to provide for your needs, and I will lead you to living holier lives."*

I could see a time coming when living at a refuge will be the safest place away from the Antichrist and the demons. Jesus said: *"My people, you are just starting to see how the persecution of Christians is getting worse, as more of your rights and freedoms are being taken away. It is Satan who is behind your death culture that is forcing abortion, euthanasia, wars, vaccines, viruses, and eventually chips in the body on your people. My faithful need to speak out against the evils of your society, but you may be persecuted for taking such a stand. This is why I am having refuges set up so My faithful could be protected. Keep fighting against evil, and you will have your reward in My Era of Peace and later in heaven."*

I could see churches being closed and more Masses will be said in the homes. Jesus said: *"My people, you will see a division coming in My Church when My faithful remnant will need to have Mass said in the homes. You can have an underground Church for awhile, but eventually you will need to come to My refuges for the safety of My angels from the evil ones, who want to kill My people. In the end I will bring My victory against all evil as they will have to bow to My power. Those, who love Me and repent of their sins, will win their crowns in heaven. Those, who refuse to love Me, and refuse to repent of their sins, will be on the way to hell."*

I could see a vision of St. Michael the Archangel as a warrior to help save America from the evil ones. St. Michael the Archangel said: *"I am Michael, and I stand before God in defense of America from all the evil that is going on in your country. I have been given authority to lead the good people against the evil ones where Our Lord will be victorious at the Battle of Armageddon. I led the good angels against the evil angels who defied God, and I drove them into hell. Another time is coming at the end of this age of the Antichrist when I will again chain Satan, the Antichrist, the False Prophet, and all the demons and evil people into hell for the last time. Rejoice in Our Lord's victory when I will lead good over evil."*

I could see all the guardian angels watching over the souls in their care. Jesus said: *"My people, you are so blessed that I love all souls in dying for your sins, and I have given each of you a guardian angel to help lead you to heaven. You all have free will to choose to love Me or not. Allow your guardian angels to help you through life's trials and temptations, so you can be with Me in heaven forever. You are challenged by your human condition, but you have My graces to strengthen you on your pilgrimage through this life. Trust in Me and stay close to Me in prayer and Confession, and you will have your reward in heaven."*

Friday, October 4, 2013: (St. Francis of Assisi)

At St. John the Evangelist after Communion, I could see the church of St. Francis in Assisi, Italy, and the birds that were constantly on his statue. St. Francis said: *"My dear little ones, you have read my story in how I gave up my family's wealth so I could be totally dependent on the Lord in directing my life in what to do. You are familiar with the order of Franciscan priests, and nuns in the cloister. You even have the Third Order Franciscans who are lay people working in the world for Jesus. I offered everything up to Jesus, even as I had the pain of the stigmata in my hands, feet, side, and head. You also have shared my stories in Assisi where I loved God's creations and the birds and animals. I even desired penance of throwing myself into the thorns of the roses, but the thorns fell off. Today, the roses in my garden do not have thorns. I gave myself to pray much, and I encouraged my followers to adopt my ways of complete surrender to Jesus. I encourage all of God's people to pray daily, and keep close to Jesus in the Mass and in frequent Confession. I am happy to see that my orders of priests and nuns have remained vigilant to my example. When you love Jesus, He will pour out His blessings on all of your activities."*

At Holy Name Divine Mercy Hour, I could see someone open a door, and in came twenty or more demons dressed in black hoods. Jesus said: *"My people, you are seeing more demons being unleashed against your country, which explains why so much evil is increasing every day. Most of your people are living in sinful lifestyles. Some are living together in fornication, while others are living in homosexual relationships. You are seeing millions of abortions and some acts of euthanasia. When your government's laws sanction these evils, this is why your punishment is at the door. You will see a division in My Church with a schismatic church teaching New Age. There will be mandatory chips in th* *where those who refuse them, will be killed. You need to call on* *have Me send down My holy angels to defend you from the demons, and from the evil ones who want to kill you. Before martial law is declared, I will warn My faithful when it is time to pack up and leave for My refuges. Your guardian angels will shield you on your way to My refuges. Trust in My protection from the demons, since evil will have a short reign before I will bring My victory over them. Then I will cast all the evil ones into hell."*

Saturday, October 5, 2013:

At Mother of Sorrows Church after Communion, I could see an old judgment seat with a purple curtain of sorrow behind it. Jesus said: *"My people, all of you will die one day, and you will have to meet Me at this judgment seat. By your actions, you will have a first judgment to heaven, hell, or purgatory. You will have My mercy, but also My justice. Nations also will have a collective judgment, but this punishment is for the sins of that nation, and it can come any time. America has helped many nations in your charity, but you will be held accountable for your sinful laws, as abortion. I have been giving America many warnings to repent of your sins, and change your evil laws. But you are not listening, nor obeying My laws. So I am telling you to be prepared for your punishment, because I will allow the one world people to take you over, and hold you as prisoners to do their will. I am providing My refuges for My faithful, so you will be protected from the evil people and the demons. Hold fast to your faith in Me, and you will share in My victory over evil."*

Later, at St. Theodore's tabernacle, I could see the wheat being harvested, and gathered into bundles. Jesus said: *"My people, the fall is the time for harvesting crops, and I am showing you how I will harvest the wheat and gather it into My barn. The chaff I will gather to be burned up in the fire. This is another portrayal of the judgment of souls. The wheat represents My faithful, and the barn represents heaven where My faithful will have their rest. The chaff represents the evil ones, and they are thrown into the eternal fire of hell. You have two choices. You can repent and obey My laws in order to come to heaven, or you can reject My love, and suffer the consequences of being in hell forever. Choose wisely, because eternity is a long time to be in the wrong place.*

I love My people, and I do everything to save your souls, even dying on the cross."

Sunday, October 6, 2013:

At Holy Name after Communion, I could see a large red light shining in front of me as a warning of some bad things to come. Jesus said: *"My people, this red light warning is to prepare My people for some bad events that will be happening in your country. You already are seeing a potential problem with your Obamacare funding, and your debt ceiling problem. If some compromises are not made soon, your financial system could go bankrupt. You will be seeing more weather disasters and people displaced from their homes. You will also be faced with a grid shutdown as a drill in November. You will be happy to see My Warning come about to give sinners a chance to prepare for the coming tribulation. Once you see mandatory chips in the body and martial law declared, you will need to come to My refuges for My protection. Trust in My angels to help you when you call on Me."*

Monday, October 7, 2013: (Our Lady of the Rosary)

At St. John the Evangelist after Communion, I could see inside the Church of the Annunciation in Nazareth where the Archangel Gabriel greeted Our Blessed Mother. The Blessed Mother said: *"My dear son,*

I am happy that you are fulfilling my plea for prayers in praying your fifteen decades of my rosary each day. Keep praying for my intentions, as I hope all of my children are listening. You have many evils going on in your world today, and more prayer is needed to balance this evil, or my Son's justice will fall upon you. I want you to give your life over to my Son's Will by carrying out your mission, and showing love to your relatives, friends, and even those people who you do not know. Reach out to help others without being asked, and you will have your reward in heaven. Encourage your family and friends to pray my rosary."

Later, at St. Theodore's tabernacle, I could see some children playing in a school yard. Jesus said: *"My people, because of your many abortions, your student population has been on the decrease. You do not see that many children in your neighborhoods. With your current economy, it is also hard to have good enough paying jobs to support bringing up your children. Many children are living in broken homes with a single parent. It is your society's moral breakdown that is causing divorce and living together without marriage, which has a bad influence on the morality of the children. It is hard enough as it is to get a college education, but single parent homes are even harder to afford such schooling. Parents also need to teach their children the faith, so they can be prepared to know, love, and serve Me in this life. You live in a world that is obsessed with addictions, but these addictions have demons attached to them. Avoid all addictions and teach your children not to allow anything to control them. When your children are nourished by your love and My love, then you can put them on the right path to heaven."*

Tuesday, October 8, 2013:

At Holy Name after Communion, I could see Jonah being called to warn Nineveh of a coming destruction. Jesus said: *"My people, the account of Jonah the prophet, shows you a rare time when the city of Nineveh was about to be destroyed, but the people repented of their sins. The king declared a fast, and the people put on sackcloth and sat in ashes in obedience to God. Because the people of Nineveh changed their sinful ways and repented, the city was spared by Me of the destruction that was intended. I am willing to forgive any repentant sinner, but the people need to show Me in their actions that they truly are changing their life of sin to be forgiven and saved. Your own mission, My son, is also one of warning the people to be prepared for the coming tribulation. Your society has been leading immoral lives of living together in fornication without marriage. They have been warned to repent, but your people are not listening, nor are they changing their sinful lives. Because they are not repenting as Nineveh did, they are calling down My justice, and your nation will be taken over, and lost to the evil one world people. If people repented and changed their life of sin, I would forgive them, and relent of My punishment. But your people are not repenting, so they will be punished for their wicked actions. I will send My Warning as a last ray of hope to convert sinners. I will also guide My faithful to places of protection at My refuges. Some will be martyred, but the rest will suffer greatly at the hands of the Antichrist, because they did not repent."*

Later, at St. Theodore's Adoration, I could see about six tribal men carrying a large animal carcass for food for the village. Jesus said: *"My people, in many of your civilizations, there is no such thing as welfare, because each person has to work for people to survive. This is how it will be at My refuges, where those, who do not work, will not be fed. Even now in your welfare society, your tax structure and the people working cannot afford to pay welfare for half the people, nor all the health care costs for half the people again. Take a look at your deficits that will grow larger with Obamacare. The average American family is living on less money than previous years, and they cannot pay enough taxes to support those not working, and still survive themselves. The one world people, who set up your debt system with the Federal Reserve, and your welfare state, knew that you would eventually go bankrupt when your debts outstripped your income. Now, you are reaching a point of insolvency, and your financial system is about to collapse. No one can run a household and survive like your government does, so be prepared for martial law, when your economy collapses under its own weight. This will be the opportunity for the one world people to take over, so be ready to leave for My refuges when the chaos and riots start."*

Wednesday, October 9, 2013: (St. John Leonardi)

At St. John the Evangelist after Communion, I could see how Jonah was dismayed that God did not punish Nineveh. Jesus said: *"My people, you need to take a lesson from Jonah's reaction both to My not punishing Nineveh, and to the gourd plant that died. When things go well, you are happy and content. But when things go against you, why do you become angry? In this account of Jonah, he may have overreacted to desire death because I did not destroy Nineveh. Even after the shade of the gourd plant was lost, he also desired death. So I ask all of you, are you angry when things do not go your way? You have been angry when your computer does not work, so you do what needs to be done to fix it. You may be angry at slow drivers, especially when you are in a hurry not to be late, so you should relax and be patient in your waiting. You may be angry when you are losing in your games, but you should realize sometimes in games of chance, you will win sometimes and lose other times. When you step back and analyze your reason for being angry, it revolves around pride and being more patient. These events in your life are more likely to displease you than favor you, so you have to be calm and understanding, and not overreact to life's disappointments as Jonah did. I am watching how you react to situations, so you need to control your emotions better for peace with yourself and others."*

Later, at St. Joseph's Place after Communion, I could see a rich person's estate with servants. Jesus said: *"My people, I do not want you to look down on anyone, no matter how important, or rich you may be. You are all equal in My eyes, so be humble and treat everyone with respect without any discrimination. You are here on this earth to serve Me out of love, and to serve your neighbor as you would want them to serve you. When you obey My laws and love everyone, you will be on the right path to heaven. In the Gospel I taught My apostles how to pray the Our Father prayer. Not only are you to love one another, but you need to forgive each other of any transgressions as well. When you pray the Our Father prayer, be willing to live out the words that you are saying. Do not just repeat words, but pray from the heart, and act out what you believe."*

At St. Theodore's Adoration, I could see an old volcano, and there was a split on its side. Then I saw a large plume of smoke and ash come rushing out the side vent much like Mt. St. Helen when it erupted. Jesus said: *"My people, a while back you had a feeling of a strong earthquake coming. Then later, you saw a 7.7 earthquake in Pakistan, and a 7.0 earthquake in Chile. Many earthquakes are related to setting off volcanoes. I am now showing you a crack in the wall of an old volcano. This was then followed by a vision of a lot of smoke and ash that gushed out of the crack, with an eruption like that of Mt. St. Helen. There are many of these disasters going on all over the world, and some like in Pakistan have destroyed a city and killed a good number of people. Pray that these disasters do not occur in heavily populated areas. Pray also that the survivors of these disasters will be able to get their lives back to normal."*

Thursday, October 10, 2013:

At Holy Name after Communion, I could see people praying to the Lord for their petitions. Jesus said: *"My people, this Gospel is teaching you to be persistent in your prayer requests, and to have faith that I will come to your aid in your needs. I know what you need before you ask, but I need to see your faith in Me so I can answer your prayers. I will always be watching over you to help you in your survival with your necessities. I will answer prayers that are best for your soul and other souls, but sometimes your worldly desires are not the best thing for your soul. You all have free will, and I do not violate that, nor do I force you to do anything. So when you pray for other souls, you need to pray for their change in spiritual disposition, so they are open to receive Me into their lives. This is what requires persistent prayer, because other souls may be under the power of the evil ones, due to their sinful behavior. Keep knocking on the doors of their souls so they can receive Me through your intercession."*

At the Eternal Father prayer group at Holy Name Adoration, I could see a snake moving about in the grass. Jesus said: *"My people, you know that the serpent is a sign of the evil one. He hides in the grass so you cannot see the evil that he is doing in tempting people to sin. Satan and the demons do not want you know that they even exist. They also do not want you to believe that there is an eternal punishment in hell. People and the demons do their evil things under the cover of darkness. This is why I shine My Light on their evil deeds so they can be seen in their sins, and they can expect to be punished if they do not repent."*

I could see a pyramid of the masons, and they were building a new Tower of Babel with a high priced stock market. Jesus said: *"My people, the evil ones, who are running your government, are the same one world people who have money as their god, and the stock market is their Tower of Babel. These financial markets are the pride of man that have rebuilt the 2008 collapse without repenting, and without asking for My help. Your dollar is like a house of cards, and it is only an owed debt that has no inherent value. Be prepared to come to My refuges when your financial system will crash or go bankrupt."*

I could see the stock market rising on news of a possible debt ceiling agreement. Jesus said: *"My people, your people and the financial markets are hoping that a deal is being made to postpone the debt ceiling deadline, even for only a short time. Opening the government will need to be worked out, but at least your leaders are trying to make a compromise in some negotiations. The gridlock in the government needs each side to get some gains or the shutdown will continue. Obamacare still needs some fixing, but these problems may take time to be resolved. Pray that the shutdown and debt ceiling can be compromised to get your government up and running. Many workers are suffering, and your credit rating lies in the balance."*

I could see several prayer groups shrinking in their memberships because our older prayer warriors are dying off. Jesus said: *"My people, I thank all of your prayer group members for being persistent in attending your weekly rosaries, because prayer is greatly needed for your evil world. Keep praying especially for the conversion of poor sinners, because I do not want to lose one soul to the evil one. For every soul who repents, all of heaven is rejoicing. Keep praying for your converts that they will remain faithful to My calling. Also pray for your relatives and friends that they may imitate your good prayer life example."*

I could see Obamacare being implemented, and it is having some initial problems in getting some insurers linked to the those people without any insurance. Jesus said: *"My people, some of the reason for your shutdown has been for some curtailing of the problems caused by Obamacare. It is just coming out in some of your media that there will be mandatory chips in the body forced on your people. You may see smart cards used at first, but there is a plan to place the mark of the beast on each citizen by having mandatory chips in the body. You are to reject any chip in the body for any reason, even if your life is threatened. These chips in the body could control your minds with voices, and they will make you into robots. Overturn this part of Obamacare, or you will need to come to My refuges of protection."*

I could see some weak family members looking up to the family prayer warriors for support and a good example. Jesus said: *"My people, My prayer warriors are My family spiritual leaders, and your family looks up to them for guidance and direction. This is why My prayer warriors need to be persistent in their faith, their daily rosaries, and their monthly Confession. Call on Me and your guardian angels to help strengthen you, so you can keep on the right path to heaven. My Blessed Mother's rosary is your most powerful weapon against the demons and breaking addictions. Your persistent prayer life is a perfect witness for helping the lukewarm and fallen away Catholics, especially in your own families."*

I could see the old Fr. Peyton movies on the Mysteries of the Rosary as he promoted: 'The family that prays together, will stay together.' Jesus said: *"My people, you can see how your families are divorcing and living together in fornication because you no longer see much family prayer. Fr. Peyton's saying is most needed in your families today. He said: 'The family that prays together, will stay together.' With each marriage I am the third partner to hold that family together. Your spouses should pray at least one rosary together and have the children pray for family unity as well. A daily commitment would be good right after supper. You will see great blessings come upon your families for making this effort to bring Me into your family life. You all have commitments, but the most important is to save the souls of your family from going to hell."*

Friday, October 11, 2013:

At St. John the Evangelist after Communion, I could see how the demons are attacking the younger generation. Jesus said: *"My people, the Gospel talks about how I cast demons out of people, and the people did not realize that I did so because I had the power of God that the demons could not fight. As you look around at your churches, you are seeing fewer young people, who have stopped coming to church and your prayer groups. The demons are especially attacking your youth because they have less supervision from their parents, and with broken homes, the youth are not following their faith that they learned in grammar school. Many of your youth are becoming addicted to drugs, alcohol, the internet, computer games, hand held devices, and living together in fornication. They have lost their moral compass, and they have become easy prey for the demons. You parents need to watch what your children are doing, and teach them good prayer habits to counter these demon attacks with their addictions. If the parents and grandparents do not look out for the souls of the youth, you will be losing a generation without any religion for themselves and their children. Keep praying for your children and grandchildren so you can help save their souls from going to hell."*

Later, at St. Theodore's Adoration, I could see a farmer on a tractor plowing and planting his fields. Jesus said: *"My people, many of you go to your stores and expect to find the food for your table with vegetables and meat products. You do not have a full appreciation of the effort involved with milk cows, pigs, and growing vegetables in the fields. You may have some small gardens, and you had to deal with bugs and rabbits that wanted to eat your crops. The farmers have even more headaches. They need to service their tractors and other machines they use. They need fertilizer, seed, and a place to store and sell their crops. They are also vulnerable to bad weather during the growing season. Pray for the success of your farmers to provide the food you need to survive. I am showing you this farm because you may need to grow some food for those people at your refuge. I know your needs, so I will multiply your food when it is necessary to feed many people. I will also help you in storing your food so it does not spoil and rot. When you are faithful to Me in prayer and deed, I will be faithful to you in providing for your needs throughout the coming tribulation. I love all of you for loving Me and helping converts. I will have My angels protect you from the evil ones at all of My refuges."*

Saturday, October 12, 2013:

At Sacred Heart Cathedral after Communion, I could see a priest raising the Host at Mass in a big church, and then he appeared transparent as his image faded away. Jesus said: *"My people, I have been showing you signs as this priest disappearing from a church, because you soon will no longer see the Mass that you know in the churches. Only the true Mass with the proper words of Consecration will be said in the homes or underground places. This is a picture of the coming division in My Church where you will see the words of Consecration changed. My Body and Blood will no longer be invoked on these altars, and you will need a faithful priest to say a proper Mass in secret. This will begin the stages of the Antichrist's coming into power, and the leader of the schismatic church will be working with him. My faithful remnant will need to seek out a private Mass with a faithful priest. I will warn My faithful when it will be time to come to My refuges where you will have My angels give you daily Holy Communion if you do not have a priest.*

Each refuge will also have Perpetual Adoration so I will always be with you during the tribulation. Be prepared to leave for My refuges with hosts and wine, as well as books and candles for Mass. Help any faithful priests who want to come with you to My refuges."

(Connie Tette Funeral Mass) At Holy Name Church after Communion, I could see Connie as a younger person. Connie said: *"I am grateful to see all of my family and friends who took the time to come to my funeral. I love all of you so very much. I thank those people who helped me in my last years. I am here with Jesus and the Blessed Mother in heaven, as I prayed to them every day to help my family. It was a joy to be a member of your prayer group, John. Give my love to Jeannie as well. I will be praying for all of you, and I will be watching out for my family members. I give praise and thanks to Jesus for the beautiful life that I had, so I could help people. Remember me in your pictures."*

Sunday, October 13, 2013:

At Holy Name after Communion, I could see some family members in need of help. Jesus said: *"My people, in today's Gospel I healed ten lepers of their leprosy, but only one returned to thank Me. I even asked, where were the other nine who did not thank Me?*

In other instances today, you may have a prayer request answered, but do you always thank Me for any healing? Every time someone helps you, you need to thank them for their service. But when I help you, you should remember even more to thank Me. You all have received some gifts of a good job, and you have at times accumulated some wealth so you can share it with others. Learn to be a good giver of both your money and your time, especially in helping your own family members. In addition to helping them financially, you can also encourage your people to come to Sunday Mass and keep close to Me in My sacraments. Saving the souls of your family members is even more important than their physical needs. Keep praying for your family to repent of their sins and to develop a good prayer life."

Monday, October 14, 2013: (St. Callistus I)

At St. John the Evangelist after Communion, I could see images of history passing by. Jesus said: *"My people, the only sign that I gave to the people of My time, was the sign of Jonah. Jonah had the mission of telling the people of Nineveh that they needed to repent of their sins, or in forty days their city would be destroyed. The people heeded his message of repentance, and the city was spared. Yet, the people of My day were given a similar message to repent by St. John the Baptist and My own mission. Some people changed and converted their lives, but not all of them, like Nineveh. I did not come to condemn the people, but I came to die for all the sins of mankind. I was telling the people also, that I was greater than Solomon or any other previous person, as seen in the vision of history. I told them that I was God the Father's Son, but they did not want to believe Me, despite all of My miracles. I am greater than any of the creatures that I created, but the people had difficulty in understanding My Incarnation as a man, who is human and Divine. This truly is a mystery to understand, as well as knowing about the mystery of the Blessed Trinity. This sign of Jonah is a sign for all the ages, as this generation. The people of the world need to repent of their sins, and change their sinful lifestyles. This is why I encourage My people to come to Confession at least once a month, so I can forgive their sins, and restore My grace to their souls. Listen to My call for repentance, and you will be on the right path to heaven."*

Later, at St. Theodore's tabernacle, I could see a small chip that will be mandatory for our Health Insurance law. Jesus said: *"My people, your original Health Care Bill had implantable chips as part of your insurance requirements. This control through digital records, is eventually going to make mandatory chips in the body a means of controlling the people's minds as well. This is the mark of the beast that I do not want My faithful to accept for any reason. Eventually, if people refuse this chip, they could be killed in death camps for not going along with the new world order. This will be enforced by a large number of foreign mercenary troops dressed in black for the UN. This is why My faithful need to have their backpacks ready to leave, when I will warn you that it is time to leave for My refuges. Your guardian angels will lead you to the nearest refuge, and you will be invisible to those who want to kill you. After the Warning, get rid of all of your electronic devices because the Antichrist will be controlling people by his image over the TV lines, and the internet. His eyes could control people's minds to worship him. Trust in Me that I will protect My people at My refuges, and I will provide for your food, water, and shelter. Be prepared to see an evil worse than ever, but the evil ones will not harm you at My refuges. Some will be martyred, but they will become instant saints."*

Tuesday, October 15, 2013: (St. Teresa of Avila)

At Holy Name after Communion, I could see a picture of St. Teresa at the foot of the stairs holding a crucifix. St. Teresa said: *"My dear son, you have had the opportunity to visit My convent in Avila, Spain. The grounds and buildings are very beautiful, and you could see by the pictures how I love my Jesus very much. I tried to instill this deep love of Jesus among my sisters in the cloister. In today's Gospel, you read how Jesus was trying to warn the Pharisees that they needed to cleanse the inside of their souls as well as washing the outside of their bodies. This is really the subject of my writings in my 'Interior Castle'. Many people and clergy have been touched by my writings to bring them closer to Jesus. You need to take quiet time with Jesus in front of His tabernacle to listen to His words to your heart. He calls all of us to be true to the mission that He has given us. We need to give our free wills over to Him so we are open to do His Divine Will. By your obedience and your good deeds, Jesus can bring you to your reward in heaven. Be patient and keep praying for sinners and the souls in purgatory every day."*

Later, at St. Theodore's tabernacle, I could see a shadow government that controlled the governments of the world. Jesus said: *"My people, I have talked about the one world people as controlling governments behind the scenes. This shadow government that I have shown you in the vision, is just another name for the one world people. These are the rich people who belong to many powerful groups as the Masons, the Bilderbergers, the Trilateral Commission, and the Council on Foreign Relations to name a few. Most all of your Cabinet members who work for your Presidents, belong to these groups. That is why no matter which party your people choose for President, the same one world people are in control. These same one world people are working to bring your country closer to bankruptcy, and they want to bring down your dollar so they can take you over. Things like shutting down the government and causing a default of the debt ceiling are all the things that these people want to cause panic and bring your government down. Pray that your legislators make some compromise to get your government up and running. If these people allow a default, then you will know who is really pulling the strings to cause a failure in your government. Once America is taken over by martial law, this will be the time to leave for My refuges. Do not hesitate, but leave promptly for My refuges with your backpacks, tents, blankets, and food and water. Trust in Me, and I will protect you from the evil ones."*

Wednesday, October 16, 2013:

At St. John the Evangelist after Communion, I could see Jesus criticizing the Pharisees and the lawyers for being hypocrites. Jesus said: *"My people, there are many people who seek fame in public places and greed for themselves, but they do not lift a finger to help other people. In the Gospel I was criticizing the Pharisees who proclaimed every Mosaic Law to the people, but they did not obey these laws themselves. When you call other people sinners, and you disobey the same laws, then you lose credibility in proclaiming My Word, since you are a hypocrite yourself. You need to clean up your own sins first by repenting in Confession, before you can proclaim My Word. In the exaggeration of the language of My day, I called people to remove the wood beam from their own eye, before they tried to remove the gnat from their brother's eye. I am the only one to truly judge someone. My faithful should leave all judging up to Me. Once you have repented of your own sins, you can make suggestions to help people to save their souls, but do not force your will or your judgment on anyone. I also criticized the lawyers for heaping heavy burdens on people while making money off of their problems. It may be just for a fair wage for their services, but lawyers make too much money in taking advantage of people, just like the tax collectors of My day who stole money from the people. You will not find very much justice among mankind, but those, who abuse the people, will have to be accountable at their judgment before Me."*

Later, at St. Theodore's Adoration, I could see a gridlock of cars that were not moving on a four lane highway. Jesus said: *"My people, this gridlock of cars on the highway is similar to the gridlock of your government shutdown and near default that just barely was averted on this last day before the deadline. Many are happy to see the government open again, but this was just a temporary agreement until January 15 for the Continuing Resolution and February 7 for the debt limit. Many of your Republicans were seeking a one year delay for individuals to sign up for Obamacare. The President and the Senate had the votes to keep Obamacare from being changed, so it was a predicted result. The House kept sending different options to the Senate, but they were all rejected by the Senate. When it came down to a possible default, the*

19

Republicans gave into voting for a Democrat bill that was disguised as a bipartisan solution. Time will reveal if the Obamacare law is a success or a failure. Some parts may be beneficial, but the cost and finding enough doctors will still be problems. Another potential problem will be if young people do not sign up, or they may pay the penalty to save money. My faithful will need to refuse this insurance when you see mandatory chips in the body forced on the people. This is when you will need to come to My refuges to protect your lives and your souls. When you see My miracles of healing and multiplication of food, you will see that My 'Jesus care' will be far better than Obamacare."

Thursday, October 17, 2013: (St. Ignatius of Antioch)
At Holy Name after Communion, I could see a defiant person standing in front of a tank in Communist China. Jesus said: *"My people, you have seen many saints who were willing to die for their faith in Me, rather than deny Me. In your society, Christians, and especially Roman Catholics, are being criticized and even persecuted for their beliefs. You stand up against abortion, euthanasia, same-sex marriage, and living together in fornication. This defiance of the immorality of your society brings problems because you affect the people's consciences by talking about the sins they are committing. These people, without morals, do not want to be told about their sins, and so they reject your righteous teaching by persecuting you and putting you down. These people do not want to admit their sins, and they do not want to repent of them either. The demons are encouraging this immoral behavior, but the people desire their sinful pleasures over loving Me. They do not want to admit they are doing wrong, so they deny that they are sinners, and attack you instead. When the immoral people see your good example, they are furious that you are against their lifestyles, and they will persecute you. It is difficult to proclaim My Word which preserves life, and encourages proper marriage without fornication, homosexual acts, nor mercy killing. My faithful need to stand up against your society's sins and evil lifestyles, even in your own families. For the sake of the souls in your family, you need to warn them of their sinful living, even if they resent you for it. You eventually will have to come to My refuges for your protection when the evil ones will want to kill you for not taking chips in the body, and not worshiping the Antichrist. You will have a choice to be a martyr, or to come to the safety of My refuges. Even if*

the evil ones capture you, you will need to be brave enough to c your faith, instead of denying Me."

Later, at the Eternal Father prayer group at Holy Name Adoration, I could see an evil picture of Satan linked with the Antichrist and the false prophet. Jesus said: *"My people, just as you are aware of the Blessed Trinity, so Satan has mocked the Blessed Trinity with an evil trinity of Satan, the Antichrist, and the false prophet. In the Blessed Trinity you have God the Father, God the Son in Me, and God the Holy Spirit. I have allowed Satan to roam the earth, and he considers the earth as part of his realm. There is a battle on earth between Satan and Me, as we are both fighting for souls. Avoid the Antichrist and do not worship him, nor look at his eyes that could control your mind. Call on My help and the angels to defend you from these evil ones."*

I could see a curtain on a stage and the actors were all dressed in white, and they acted like the living dead. Jesus said: *"My people, when people live in mortal sin, their souls are dead to Me without any grace. This can be changed when these people come to Confession, and they are forgiven of their sins. Then their souls are beaming with grace. A new evil is coming when you will have mandatory chips in your body according to your Health Insurance Law. People, who knowingly take this chip and worship the Antichrist, will also be among the living dead because they will be hypnotized by voices to be like robots with their free will controlled by evil beings. Refuse to take any chip in the body, and refuse to worship the Antichrist, even if they threaten your life or take all of your money."*

I could see the sun turn black as with an eclipse and there was a great display in the sky on the day of the Warning. Jesus said: *"My people, on the day of the Warning, you will see a great display in the sky that could frighten some souls. At that point all of the souls will come out of their bodies and be outside of time, all at the same time for everyone. You will come through tunnels of time to see My Light. When you are before Me, you will have an illumination of your conscience as you will have a life review of all of your actions. You will not only be reminded of your actions, but you will also witness them from the viewpoint of the people who you helped or harmed, as well as from My viewpoint. You will be judged to heaven, hell, or purgatory, and then you will be given a second chance to improve your lives when you are placed back into your bodies. Pay attention to this Warning because it may be the last chance to save some souls. It will also be coming sooner than you think.*"

I could see some people preparing food and shelters for the coming possible riots of a revolution. Jesus said: "*My people, it is one thing to be prudent and put aside some extra food and money to get through some bad times. It is another thing to trust in Me to provide for your needs. Do not worry about saving your life on earth, for the body will die and turn back into dust. Instead, work with Me to save your soul because your soul lives on forever. You would much rather spend all eternity with Me in heaven with the One who loves you, instead of being with Satan forever in hell with the one who hates you. Keep your focus on Me in your daily prayers and monthly Confession, and you will see your reward in heaven.*"

I could see an exposition of unborn baby models at various months of development. Jesus said: "*My people, your right to life groups have displayed these baby models at various months so you realize this is a living human baby throughout all nine months of development. Some people may criticize these displays, but it may help women to see what their baby looks like at the time of their abortion. It is an opportunity to help those women who had abortions so they could be consoled in their sin, and point them to My loving arms as I await their seeking of My forgiveness in Confession. You pray to stop abortions, and you pray for these mothers who aborted their children. Life is precious, and it should be valuable to everyone.*"

I could see all of the preparations being made for Halloween and all the ghosts and witches that are portrayed in these decorations. Jesus said: "*My people, I do not want you to glorify Halloween that appears to glorify evil, even more than My birth at Christmas. The children may want to go out to gather some candy from generous people. This is really a bad influence on your children to glorify demons, witches and ghosts. Instead of dressing the children up in evil costumes, let them be dressed as saints because it is the eve of All Saints' Day. Do not give any credit to evil, but glorify heavenly beings as the saints, who by their lives, are a good example to imitate.*"

I could see some winter snow storms and some severe flooding out West. Jesus said: "*My people, at times you see people killed or made homeless by weather disasters of snow and floods. When something happens to you, you are more understanding of how you can lose your home. You can make some donations to help people with disasters, either with money or food. You also can make donations to your local food shelves where you know how your money is used. When you reach out to help people, you will gain merits in heaven, and your heart will feel satisfied that you helped someone."*

Friday, October 18, 2013: (St. Luke)

At St. John the Evangelist after Communion, I could see Jesus sending out His disciples to spread the Word of the Kingdom of God. Jesus said: *"My people, I have chosen My disciples who I wanted to spread My Word. They all had to say 'yes' to the mission that I was giving them. I told them to not take much with them because My laborer is deserving of his keep. Even as I called My disciples in My time on earth, I call other prophets and messengers for these end times as well. Not only did I chose you, but you gave Me your 'yes' as well. Unless people give their consent to do My Will, then it is difficult to fulfill their mission because the devil will distract them. My evangelists also require a deep love for Me in a daily prayer life. They also need to keep close to Me in at least monthly Confession and frequent visits in front of My tabernacle. You need a quiet space by Me to hear My voice, and remove all of the worldly distractions. Once you are focused on Me, then I can share My Word of love to My people. My evangelists also must be ready to travel to spread My Word, and they may suffer pains or endure disappointments on their way. These things are to build up your spiritual strength so you can fight off the temptations of the evil one. Pray for safe travel, and sprinkle some holy water or blessed salt on your vehicle. When you pray, I will send My angels to guard your way to keep you safe. I thank all of My servants who go forth to all the nations to spread My Word of the Kingdom of God."*

Later, at St. Peter's Adoration Chapel, at Mt. Clemens, Michigan I could see a door open and a young bishop walked out. Jesus said: *"My people, because all of your bishops have to retire at seventy-five years old, you are seeing many dioceses across your country that are in need of a new bishop. In your own Diocese of Rochester, New York, you are also in need of a new bishop. When you saw a young bishop walk out, this was a sign that you would be getting a new bishop, but it could take some time. It is how a bishop runs his diocese that will either enhance the people's faith, or it may result in more schools and churches closing.*

... ...e faith in a diocese is as strong as its leadership. You have seen how I sent out My disciples to evangelize the people. In today's society it will be the faithful laity that will help save the people from their sins. There is still a faithful remnant that has prayer groups, attends Masses, and prays daily. You may see them in My Adoration chapels, or in the Confession lines. These traditional Catholics are an inspiration to the children. One example of tradition is when you visit three or more churches on Holy Thursday night in Holy Week of Lent. If My faithful remained true to their younger upbringing, you would not have all of the divorces and separations in the families. You would also have fuller churches on Sunday, and longer lines at Confession. As it is now, you are seeing more people leaving the Church, and very few are praying. The Confession lines are smaller as well. Keep praying for a renewal in My Church that newly installed bishops could help inspire."

Saturday, October 19, 2013:

At San Francesco Church at Clinton Township, Michigan after Communion, I could see a door leading to a wine cellar with many bottles stored on a wall. Jesus said: *"My people, in the Mass you use bread and wine that are consecrated by the priest into My Body and Blood. But there are some people who want to drink too much wine, and they can become drunk with alcohol. Once you drink too much alcohol, you do not have control of your mind and your senses. Some even get violent in such a state of drunkenness. Drinking a little is appropriate, but drinking to excess becomes sinful because of your lack of control, especially when you are driving. If you drink and drive, you are endangering the lives of others on the road. Those, who drink to excess often, can become addicted to alcohol, and they become alcoholics. Remember also that there are demons connected to such addictions. It is not easy to heal an alcoholic because their craving for alcoholic drinks is hard to ignore. If someone wants to be healed, it takes a personal choice to stop and get help. It also takes prayer and fasting to deal with the demon or demons that are controlling this person. To heal alcoholics you cannot enable them by giving them money or access to alcoholic drinks. It takes tough love to help them, but if they do not want to help themselves, your job will be more difficult. Not only does drinking endanger a person's health, but it also endangers the soul that a person could lose to the demons in hell. When you have someone with this addiction in your family, you need to pray and fast to cast out these demons. Help these people the most that you can, because they can cause much harm to those people around them. Addictions are one of the worst threats to your soul, so work to not allow anything to control you."*

Sunday, October 20, 2013:
At the Immaculate Conception Church, Anchorville, Michigan after Communion, I could see a crucifix and a cross in front of a grave. Jesus said: *"My people, all the time in heaven My saints and angels are giving*

Me praise and Adoration. I know that My people are weak and distracted easily in your human condition. Still I want My people to do as the saints and angels do, and give Me praise and glory every day. Today's Gospel speaks about persevering in prayer for your intentions and about faith in Me to heal people and answer their prayers. There are many ways to pray, and when you pray, you are talking directly to My Heart. The five types of prayer are: prayers of worship as at Mass, prayers of Adoration as when you pray before My monstrance or tabernacle, prayers of petition as when you pray for people's souls, prayers of thanksgiving as when you are thanking Me for favors received, and

prayers of blessings as when you pray grace before meals. In the vision you are seeing a crucifix in front of a grave. This has two meanings. The first meaning is how each soul can prepare for its death by becoming united with Me in daily prayer and a love relationship that will save this soul for heaven. The second meaning is how My faithful can pray for the deceased that may still have their souls in purgatory. Your Masses and prayers for the souls in purgatory can gain their release so they can come to heaven quicker."

Later, at St. Anastasia Adoration Chapel, Sterling Heights, Michigan, I could see an upside down scene of an occult meeting being carried out in a forest. Jesus said: *"My people, I am giving you a warning that the demons and evil people do not like your messages that are revealing their dark secrets. I told you that when you pray over people in your binding of the demons prayer, that you could see a push back from the demons. This could take many forms of attack, but you have already seen attacks before, as the car in the wrong lane, your flat tire in the dark, and the major accident when someone ran a red light and hit you. So keep praying your St. Michael prayer and invoke My protection as you drive your car. My power is more powerful than all of the demons, so call on Me and My angels to protect you. Have no fear of the demons, and trust in My protection."*

Monday, October 21, 2013: (Kevin Zaleski Funeral Mass)

At Mary, Queen of Creation Church, New Baltimore, Michigan after Communion, I could see someone opening a Bible as a way of life. Jesus said: *"My people, it is always sad to see a younger person die before their time. Pray for Kevin in this time of mourning. I showed you a Bible in the vision as a way of life in following My Word. Even the priest reminded you of your early teaching of why you are here on earth to know, love, and serve Me. You can come to know Me in reading the Scriptures, and witnessing My creation. You can love Me in your daily prayers, and receiving Me in Holy Communion. You can serve Me by helping your neighbor in their needs, both in the body and helping the soul with your good example. Your prayer groups give you an opportunity to share your faith in your rosaries and your faith fellowship. Thank Me for the gift of Kevin's life in all of your lives. He loves you all so much."*

Later, at the Holy Martyrs Chaldean Church, Sterling Heights,

Michigan at Mass, I could see a weeping Fatima Statue. The Blessed Mother said: *"My dear children, many of you are curious why my*

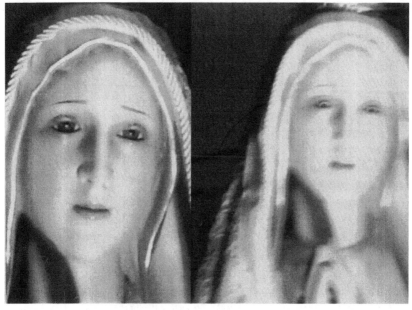

statue is weeping oil here. This miracle is a testimony to the faith of the people at this church that honors me in my traveling Statue of Fatima. I am crying tears in various places in America because your sins of abortion are greatly offending my Son, Jesus. I am making a request of my children to pray for the stoppage of abortion in your country. Do whatever you can to show the people how evil it is to kill your unborn children. My Son has warned you in many messages to stop this killing, or you will see His hand of justice fall against America. Pray, pray, pray, to stop your abortions in America." Note: Our friend Kathy took a picture of the statue, and then asked the Blessed Mother to give her a miraculous picture, since she never had one. When she took another picture, we could see a brightness come through her cell phone. Mary is obviously more sorrowful for our sins of abortion.

(Reparation Mass)At Immaculate Conception Church, Anchorville, Michigan after Communion, I could see a round window on the wall. It was dark outside, and I could see the dark clouds of the tribulation about to descend on us. Jesus said: *"My people, I have talked to you before about your choice between loving Me or your money. I also want My faithful to be able to share their wealth with others. In the Bible there is a recommendation of tithing your income so you can give ten percent of your income to support My Church and your charities. This vision shows you that the tribulation is almost upon you. Do not concern yourself with accumulating this world's wealth because it is temporary, and in a short time your dollar will be worthless. Even gold and silver will not buy you anything without a chip in the body. Be more concerned with building up your treasure in heaven because your soul lives on forever, but your body will pass away just like your wealth. Your prayers and good deeds will help store treasure in heaven, so focus more on helping your neighbor than your own needs that I will help you with on earth, and later in My Era of Peace."*

Tuesday, October 22, 2013: (Blessed John Paul II)
At San Francesco Church, Clinton Township, Michigan after Communion, I could see a large bridge where all the people could travel. This was a sign that Jesus made a bridge for us to heaven. Jesus said: *"My people, you are aware that by the sin of Adam and Eve, all of mankind has inherited original sin and all the consequences of this sin. This is why you have to die, and it is why you are weak to committing sin. I did not leave mankind orphans, but I promised all of you a Redeemer. This is why I was incarnated as a God-man. Through My Blessed Mother, I was born into this world so I could offer Myself up as a perfect unblemished sacrifice. This is how I could ransom all of the souls of mankind in the past, present, and the future. By the grace of My death on the cross, I can offer all of you the salvation of your souls, and I can offer you the opportunity of coming to heaven. If you open your hearts and souls to Me in love and follow My Commandments, then I will open the gates of heaven to welcome you to your heavenly reward. The Gospel speaks of having your soul always purified by frequent Confession so you are always ready to meet Me at your judgment, whenever you should die. I want all of you to be prepared, even if you should die this day. By keeping your soul pure, following My Commandments, and performing good deeds for your neighbor, you will be found worthy of heaven. Of those souls who are saved, some may have to be purified in purgatory. This is why I ask My faithful to pray for the deceased and have Masses said for their souls. In this way souls can be released from purgatory for heaven. I love all of you so much that I died to save your souls. All*

you need to do is accept My gift of salvation, and follow My Will.''

Later, at St. Theodore's Adoration, I could see a young girl pointing out a man who sexually abused her. Jesus said: *"My people, you have heard about some priests who committed pedophilia acts on young boys. There also have been men caught molesting young girls of all ages. It becomes even a worse crime when parents or other relatives have sex with young girls or young boys in their own family. Sometimes these molestations are kept secret, but some family members suspect this behavior, or the child could reveal it to some member. The parent or relative should know their actions are sinful, and they should have it forgiven in Confession. Pray for the children who are molested, so it does not harm them later in life when they get married. If this incident happens often, it could damage the children's trust in their parents or relatives if it is allowed to continue. Pray for your children that they are not abused by anyone. These little ones are precious in My eyes, and I do not want to see them harmed in any way.''*

Wednesday, October 23, 2013: (St. John of Capistrano)

At St. John the Evangelist after Communion, I could see the farmers gathering hay and grain for the harvest. Jesus said: *"My people, St. Paul shows you that you were once slaves of sin, but now that you are converted to following Me, you are slaves of righteousness. You all should follow My Commandments if you wish to be with Me in heaven. When you walk in My ways, then you will be living in My grace. My faithful have learned much from Me, and you have received many gifts to help you with your mission to reach out and save souls. Because you have been given much, much more will be expected of you in using your gifts. You are in the Fall season of the harvest, and the farmers have to cut and gather the hay at the proper time when the hay is dry, so it will not have mold as it is stored. This physical harvest is symbolic of the spiritual harvest of souls at the end of this age. This will be a time of judgment of souls when they will be held accountable for their life's actions. Keep in mind that you are all good people, but it is your deeds that will either condemn you, or bring you merits for heaven. Keep focused on Me, and do everything for My greater glory, and not for your glory.''*

Later, at St. Theodore's Adoration, I could see an aisle in a restaurant where people were eating their breakfast. Jesus said: *"My people, many of you go out to restaurants, and you expect them to have plenty of food to sell. In the same way, you go to grocery stores, and you are spoiled with so many choices of food. When all is going well, you can live comfortably with plenty of food available. There are times when you have disasters of tornadoes, floods, and snow storms. In these cases it might be harder to find food that has not been damaged. I have warned My faithful to stock up on some extra food and fuel for when your stores might be closed, or when you may need a chip in the body to buy your food. You have seen the stores get cleared out when there is an impending disaster. Being prepared with food to eat, and fuel to keep warm, may help the body. Being prepared spiritually involves having a good prayer life, and a pure soul with frequent Confession. Having some blessed sacramentals can also protect you from the demons. As you get closer to the declaration of the Antichrist, you will especially want to be prepared, so you can come to the safety of My refuges. Your bodies and your souls will be at risk, so call on My help and My angels to put My shield of invisibility over all of you."*

Thursday, October 24, 2013: (St. Anthony Claret)
At St. John the Evangelist after Communion, I could see a wave of water representing the need to cleanse our sins so we can receive Holy Communion worthily. Jesus said: *"My people, in the reading from St. Paul to the Romans he proclaimed: 'For the wages of sin is death, but the gift of God is life everlasting in Christ Jesus Our Lord.'* (Romans 6:23) *It is important to realize that satisfying the body's cravings in sinful behavior, will take you away from the One you love. Do not offend Me with such things, when you could be showing Me your love in obedience to My Commandments. These earthly pleasures are fleeting, and they only will draw you to repeat these sins. You will never have peace in sin because I am the only One who can bring peace to your soul. In the Gospel I spoke of bringing division between your family members. This is not an intended division because I truly want My people to be united in love of Me. But when I bring My love and a desire for your obedience to My laws, not all of your family members will believe, and have a strong love for Me. Some will be weak, and they may not come to Sunday Mass, nor frequent Confession. If you truly love Me, you will seek to avoid sinful behavior, and seek My forgiveness when you fall into sin. Keeping a pure soul requires some spiritual effort, and*

not all of your members may be willing to make this commitment. So those of you who are faithful, could be at odds with those who do not love Me. This is another sign of the battle of good against evil. Strive to be a good example to the weak souls, and work to convince them that following Me will bring them eternal life in heaven."

Later, at the Eternal Father prayer group at Holy Name Adoration, I could look up and see the dome in the rotunda of the Capitol. Jesus said: *"My people, there are plans to repair the Capitol building where the Congress conducts its business. Some of your people would say your government is in need of repair because of the major gridlock that is occurring over many issues in your Congress. I understand that some people are against Obamacare because the government is forcing everyone to buy health insurance. The start of this huge program has had a lot of problems in signing up with some computer problems. Now, your Health Department is giving you a month or so reprieve from paying any penalties. This program needs a major repair as well, and the people have yet to see what premiums they will be paying."*

I could see some related problems with Obamacare. Jesus said: *"My people, some people do not like the fact that everyone is not treated fairly with Obamacare. The big businesses, Congress, and the unions are getting special waivers that allowed a one year delay in implementing Obamacare. Small businesses and other individuals do not have waivers, and they are having problems signing up for this health insurance. It appears that this whole program should be postponed until the sign up problems are corrected."*

I could see a big binder that stored my messages. Jesus said: *"My dear son, ever since you elected to journal My messages, you have been storing these messages in a large binder so you can have easy access to showing people. You also type them up, and you send them to your spiritual director every two weeks. This requires a lot of typing, and you have been faithful to this labor of love that provides a digital form for the internet and the books at Queenship Publishing Company. I thank you for all that you are doing to fulfill this mission."*

I could see a rainbow of colors that could be seen in the rain when the sun was shining. Jesus said: *"My people, the rain acts as a prism which breaks down your white light into many different colors. This rainbow shows red, orange, yellow, green, blue, indigo, and violet. This was a covenant given to Noah after the flood that stated I will not bring such a flood on the world again. There are other covenants that I have made such as promising mankind a Redeemer which was fulfilled in My death on the cross. I am faithful to My Word, and I would like a similar promise by man to be faithful to following My Commandments. I have given you the sacrament of Penance to make reparation for when you disobey My laws. See My love in everything that I do to bring your souls to heaven."*

I could see how Right to Life groups are struggling to get out the message of saving the babies from abortion. Jesus said: *"My people, there is a political battle going on between those who favor abortion, and those who are fighting to save the babies in the womb from being killed by abortion. Your Right to Life groups are run mostly by volunteers and what donations they can get from the people. This is a small amount of money compared to taxpayer money that goes to Planned Parenthood. You can add your voice as an advocate for the defenseless little babies in the womb that they may be protected from being killed."*

I could see a dark shadow over America that represented the death culture that is led by Satan. Jesus said: *"My people, the death culture is sponsored by Satan and those who worship him. Many of the high levels of masons and other one world groups actually worship Satan and take his orders to kill man. These people are the ones killing babies in abortion, killing older people with euthanasia, killing your people in wars, and they are killing people with viruses and vaccines. This is why it is hard to fight them in their evil deeds because they have money and political power on their side. My people have Me on their side, and I will open doors so they can be effective in fighting these evil ones who do everything for money as their god."*

I could see the twenty-one Missions that we visited a while back. Jesus said: *"My faithful pilgrims, you will be embarking on another pilgrimage to these old mission churches in California. You remember the first message that I gave you at the beginning of your trip which asked for prayers for those who would be killed in the coming earthquakes. You are doing special Masses of reparation for this same cause. Continue praying for all those who are killed in disasters when these souls are not fully prepared to meet Me at their judgment. With your continuous prayers and Masses, I will have mercy on such souls who did not have time to purify their souls beforehand."*

Friday, October 25, 2013:

At a lady's house for Adoration, Saskatoon, Saskatchewan, Canada, I could see a long train coming. It was not a sign for taking people to heaven, but it was a sign of us being taken to refuges. Jesus said: *"My people, I have been preparing My people for when the persecution will*

be so great that it will be necessary for your guardian angels to lead you to the nearest refuge. This coming train in the vision is a sign that this time to leave is close. I have also inspired a good number of faithful who have given Me their 'yes' to working on their own refuge. This is not an easy decision because it takes some work and a commitment to preparing a place for the people to come. It would be ideal for every refuge to be consecrated by a priest, and to have an independent source of water. At many refuges people are storing food supplies and fuel that could be multiplied to accommodate the people. Some are setting up dormitories for sleeping and possible farms for producing their own crops. You will see My angels protecting each refuge from any evil people. The bigger refuges will have My luminous cross in the sky for the people to be healed of all of their ailments when they look on the cross. Have faith and trust in Me when I will protect My people. Some will be martyred, but they will become instant saints. This tribulation of the Antichrist will be your purgatory on earth. Rejoice that you will see My victory over the evil ones in your lifetime. This is an exciting time to live when I will prune all of your earthly attachments, so you can come into a fuller love of your Savior. You will have perpetual Adoration at all of My refuges. Many beautiful souls love to come and bask in My graces and in My Light with My Blessed Sacrament."

Later, at Luc and Cecil's house after Communion, I could see a tall vine as a tree that represented Jesus, and we are the branches. Jesus said: *"My people, I am the Vine, and you are the branches. All of those people, who love Me and obey My Commandments, are a part of Me in the Communion of Saints. Those people, who reject Me, fall away from the Vine and they scatter. I am the One who gives you nourishment in My sacraments, and My faithful will have eternal life with Me in heaven. This choice of choosing Me or not, is part of the battle between the spirit and the body. By fasting and prayer you can strengthen your spirit in order to resist the desires of the body. In the Gospel I am showing you that you can read the signs of weather to know whether you will have a nice day or a stormy day. In the same way I want you to be able to read the signs of your times. In the Bible I have described the end times in more severe earthquakes, famine, and pestilence. You are seeing these signs with more earthquakes and viruses that are killing the people. You are living in the end times as you see evil being allowed to have abortions, euthanasia, same sex marriage, and living together in fornication. This increase in evil and this increase in knowledge are further signs of the end times. The Antichrist is about to declare himself, and bring about the tribulation. I will protect My faithful at My refuges, so have no fear of the evil ones."*

Saturday, October 26, 2013:

At St. Louis Church, St. Louis, Saskatchewan, Canada after Communion, I could see a scene of Jesus praying on a rock in the Garden of Gethsemane. Jesus said: *"My people, this scene of My agony in the Garden of Gethsemane is familiar to you about prayer. I had asked My apostles to pray with Me, but they fell asleep at night. I came back to them the third time, and I told them: 'Could you not pray one hour with Me?' I am always telling My people not to get so caught up in their*

earthly distractions, so they can make some time for Me in prayer. When you pray, do not just repeat words, but pray from the heart because I hear all of your prayers and petitions. I have told you in the past that if you do not keep up a good prayer life, then you could lose some of your gifts. I commend My people who are also adamant in attending your prayer groups. When you give your 'yes' to Me, you can share your faith with others, especially at your prayer groups. In the morning consecrate your whole day's activities over to Me, and then everything that you do for Me will be like a prayer. You also need to instill a good prayer life in your children and grandchildren. It is important to pass your faith on to the next generation so they can pass it on to their children. Remember that it is important to keep praying for your relatives and friends because you could be the grace to save their souls from hell, even though some are not coming to Church on Sunday. Working to save souls should be your most important mission."

Sunday, October 27, 2013:

At St. Michael's Church, Prince Albert, Saskatchewan, Canada after Communion, I could see people greeting others into their home to share a meal. Jesus said: *"My people, today's Gospel speaks about having humility instead of boasting of your own goods and talents. I do not want you to judge or discriminate other people so you treat everyone the same. I see all of you as equal in My eyes, and I look into your heart to understand the motivation behind your actions. You may fool others with your outward actions, but I know all of your secret intentions behind what you do. I ask all of you to be loving of everyone, even your enemies or those whom you dislike. You all are made in My image, and you all are capable of loving Me and each other. I want My people to reach out in love to help their neighbors in their needs, and even to share their faith with them. You can share your money, your goods, and your time in using your talents to help others. Even when you help others, do everything without expecting repayment because you give everything out of love. You can also pray for people in helping souls, and give them a good example as a Christian should. As you pray and ask My forgiveness of your sins out of humility, then you too can go home justified by the proper intentions in your heart. The more you share with others, the more merits and treasure that you are storing up in heaven for your day of judgment."*

Later, at St. Michael's Adoration, Prince Albert, Saskatchewan Canada, I could see a priest putting incense on a charcoal and incensing the Blessed Sacrament. Jesus said: *"My people, I desire that you give Me proper reverence in My Blessed Sacrament. You remember when I asked St. Peter three times if he loved Me. He said that he did love Me, and I said: 'Feed My sheep'. I ask all of My people: 'Do you love Me?' If you truly love Me, then you could show that love by your actions in revering My Real Presence. When you receive Me in Holy Communion, make sure you are free of any mortal sin, so you do not commit any sin of sacrilege. When you come into church at your pew, you could genuflect to My tabernacle.*

Those souls, who truly love Me in My Blessed Sacrament, could come to adore Me before the monstrance or My tabernacle in their holy hour visits. Not only could you show Me reverence, but you could teach your children and grandchildren to also have reverence for My Real Presence in My Blessed Sacrament. If you bring yourself to honor Me, I will honor you before My heavenly Father. Keep your focus on Me every day so you can be close to Me in love for all that you do."

Monday, October 28, 2013:

At St. Isidore's tabernacle, Bellvue, Saskatchewan, Canada, I could see rural land and a refuge. Jesus said: *"My people, I have been preparing My people to be able to leave their homes to come to My refuges when their lives and souls will be endangered by the evil ones. When you come to a refuge, you will be fortunate to have electricity, if you have solar power. You were given a little test this morning when the grid power went off for a few hours. You learned to deal with the cold with your wood stove, and you needed candles for your light source. If you had no electricity, you would have to deal more with heating, lighting, and rare warm water. You have been spoiled with many convenient devices, but you will be living a more rustic life with more time for your prayers. My angels will protect you from the evil ones, but you will be using root cellars to store your food. I will send you daily Communion with My angels, and deer for meat. Your lives will be different for only a brief reign of the Antichrist. Rejoice when I will bring My victory over the evil ones, and I will bring My people into My Era of Peace, and later into heaven."*

Later, at Luc and Cecil's house during the rosary, I could see two buildings close to each other. Jesus said: *"My people, I have given missions to everyone in addition to bringing up children for couples. There are many trials in providing a home, and securing adequate employment to support the families. Some people have been called to have special places to help others during the tribulation. I commend My holy workers who have dedicated themselves to be ready to help their neighbors with food and lodging. I bless Luc and Cecil for all that they are doing for Me and others."*

Tuesday, October 29, 2013:

At St. Theodore's Adoration, I could see a transfigured Jesus glowing in a bright Light in the middle of a wheat field. Jesus said: *"My people, you have just seen the harvest of the wheat which represents My faithful at the judgment. The wheat of My faithful is gathered into My barn of heaven, and the chaff is collected, and these evil souls are burned in hell for their evil deeds. These faithful make up My Communion of Saints among the obedient souls on earth in the Church militant, the souls in purgatory in the Church suffering, and the saints in heaven in the Church triumphant. During November you make a remembrance of all the people who died in the last year. You will soon be celebrating All Saints day on November 1ˢᵗ and All Souls day on November 2ⁿᵈ, when you pray for the souls in purgatory. You remember how the souls that have been separated from their bodies want you to have their pictures displayed as a remembrance of their lives among you. Sometimes these souls in purgatory are allowed to give signs that they need your prayers and Masses to get out of purgatory, and come to heaven. During November remember to pray for your deceased relatives who may still be suffering in purgatory. Also pray for all the souls in purgatory, especially for those souls whom no one is praying for them."*

Wednesday, October 30, 2013:

At St. John the Evangelist after Communion, I could see a long tapestry with pictures of a person's life and a bright Light of Jesus at the end of it. Jesus said: *"My people, at a funeral you see many collages of pictures of that person's life. When all of you will face your Warning experience, it will be like a near death experience. Just as at a funeral, you will see flashes of the various pictures of your life, only you will see it like a movie from the perspective of other people, and My viewpoint. I will let you know what is true right and wrong, and you will be judged according to your actions and My laws. At the end of your life review, you will be able to remember every unforgiven sin so you could tell it in Confession. Then you will receive a mini-judgment to heaven, hell, or purgatory. Each person will visit where the judgment was given to know that these places exist, and what it would be like at that destination. This life review will occur outside of your body and outside of time for everyone at the same time. Then you all would return to your bodies to change your lives, and repent of your sins. If you do not change or improve your life, then your mini-judgment will become your final judgment. This Warning experience is a wake-up call for all sinners to see where their lives are headed. It may be the last chance to save some souls, so you will be working hard to convert your family members who will be more open to your evangelization efforts. Give praise and thanks to My Divine Mercy for allowing all sinners to have a second chance to save their souls."*

Later, at St. Theodore's Adoration, I could see someone suffering in pain. Jesus said: *"My people, there are a lot of people suffering in pain from various health problems. Use this opportunity to offer up your pain to Me as a redemptive merit for souls in purgatory or souls on earth. There is a lot of pain being wasted, when it could be offered up to help someone. Not everyone realizes that they could help other souls. So no matter how little or how great your pain is, remember to offer it up for your relatives and friends either for those deceased or those who are alive. You can also offer up your prayers and Masses for the same intentions. Many souls who are going to hell, could be helped by your pleading for their souls to be saved. Keep struggling to save souls who could be lost without your help."*

Thursday, October 31, 2013:
At Holy Name after Communion, I could see money in someone's back pocket. Jesus said: *"My people, I want all of My faithful to be generous in sharing their wealth in supporting My Church, and their charities. In the Scriptures it is said that I love a cheerful giver without holding back with any selfishness. When you can afford to be generous, you could even tithe in your giving of ten percent of your income. There are many deserving causes to contribute to, especially if your own family needs help. As you approach Thanksgiving Day, you could share a donation with your local food shelf in helping the poor to have something to eat. You could also share your time, talent, and faith in helping souls to be saved. I have given many people more than enough to live on, so you could share some of your excess wealth. Think of giving financially as a way of thanking Me for all of the blessings that I have given you."*

Later, at the Eternal Father prayer group at Holy Name Adoration, I could see inside a whale as Jonah was spewed up on the shore by the whale. Jesus said: *"My people, I told the people of My day that the only sign that I would give, is the sign of Jonah. Even in this present world, I give the same sign of Jonah. At the call of Jonah for the people of Nineveh to repent of their sins, the people put on sackcloth and ashes, and they repented of their sins. Because these people repented, I spared them the punishment I had intended. But America is not repenting of its sins, nor is it stopping its abortions or evil laws. Because of the evil being done in America, your country will see one disaster after another, until the one world people will take you over. Trust in Me to protect My faithful from the evil ones."*

I could see more taxes coming over everyone from Obamacare. Jesus said: *"My people, while your government promised everyone access to health insurance, they did not tell you about all the new taxes that will burden the middle class. Many people are having their old insurance dropped because it did not meet all the requirements of Obamacare. Some companies are canceling their health plans or they are reducing forty-hour workers to thirty-hour workers. Between the high costs and* the doctors leaving, implementing Obamacare could have some large problems for health care. Trust in My care that you will eventually have at My refuges."

I could see a farm at a refuge where people were feeding their animals. Jesus said: *"My people, some refuges have farms for cows, rabbits, chickens, and other animals for food. The feed and fuel for these farms will have to be multiplied to keep their animals alive. My people will have food as deer that will be provided, but you will need people to butcher the meat and prepare it for the people to have food to eat. Vegetables and fruit trees will be farmed to provide a balanced meal. Trust that I will provide for your needs, but people will be needed to prepare and serve the meals."*

I could see the saints and angels looking down on us on earth. Jesus said: *"My people, tomorrow is All Saints Day and it is a time to recognize all the saints in heaven, even those who have not been canonized by My Church. The saints are to be imitated in your lives as you struggle toward being a saint in heaven. Many of you will need purifying either in purgatory or during the tribulation on earth. I will not test you beyond your endurance, but you will be tried in this tribulation with much persecution. Remain strong in your faith, and you will have your reward in heaven."*

I could see the souls suffering in purgatory who need our prayers and Masses. Jesus said: *"My people, the souls in upper purgatory do not have My loving Presence, but they do not suffer the pain of the flames. In lower purgatory, souls suffer from not seeing Me, and they suffer a burning from the flames that causes them pain. They suffer an inner pain in their souls without their bodies. This is why these souls are crying out for your prayers and Masses, so they can be relieved of their suffering. Do not forget to pray for these souls, especially on All Souls' Day."*

I could see some evil worship and vandalism that occurs on All Saints' Eve or Halloween. Jesus said: *"My people, this day is an evil holiday for many occult groups. Those people, who worship Satan, are influencing many people adversely out of curiosity in the occult. Such worship and taking evil potions can allow demons to possess people. Pray for all souls to wake up if they are delving in occult practices as New Age and Wicca. Pray for My precious Blood to be poured over these souls so they can be predisposed to My love."*

I could see the darkness of Halloween overcome by the Light of

Jesus on All Saints' Day. Jesus said: *"My people, even though evil will have a brief reign, I will bring My victory over evil with My Comet of Chastisement. The tribulation will be shortened for the sake of My elect. All the demons and evil people will be cast into hell at the coming judgment. Rejoice that you will be receiving your reward in My Era of Peace and later in heaven. You will see a Battle of Armageddon where the good side will be victorious over the evil side."*

Friday, November 1, 2013: (All Saints Day)

At St. John the Evangelist after Communion, I could see the apostles with a single flame of the Holy Spirit over each of them. Jesus said: *"My people, today you are celebrating All Saints Day as you give honor to all the canonized saints, and all the unknown saints who have made it to heaven. The saints are your heroes who you could imitate in following their lives to holiness in your own lives. The saints are your models to follow on your own way to a crown of sainthood in heaven. You may think in your weakness that it would be hard to become a saint. On your own, it would be very difficult, but with My help and grace, all things are possible. You need to be perfect like a saint to enter heaven, but you are not perfected all at once. It is a struggle to remain faithful through all the devil's temptations. You may fall into sin at times, but you need to pick yourselves up and confess your sins to the priest in Confession. I have given you My sacraments to strengthen you through this evil world. By prayers and your daily sacrifices, you can keep focused on Me and on your goal of sainthood in heaven."*

Later, at Holy Name Divine Mercy Hour, I could see the trees down on some power lines. Jesus said: *"My people, you just witnessed very high winds that took trees down, and some houses and and businesses were without electricity. When damage is reported on your news, you pray for the people to recover. When your own heavy tree limbs fell down in your own yard, it becomes more of a difficulty in picking up the trees and branches. In some cases falling trees can damage fences, cars, and even homes. When the trees fall on your power lines, it can create power outages in wide areas. So now when you hear about tornado or hurricane damage, you can be more sympathetic for what these people have to endure. You were fortunate this time that it was not very cold. You can remember the problems with heating your house and with lights when you had an ice storm that took eleven days to restore power.*

These are some of the trials that you face every day. Give thanks to Me for all the other times when you have no power outages."

Saturday, November 2, 2013: (All Souls Day)
At Mother of Sorrows Church after Communion I could see souls in purgatory suffering in the flames with a prison door keeping them from coming out. Then I saw a soul's judgment, and they headed into a fall into the abyss of purgatory. Jesus said: *"My people, I am merciful, but I am just as well. Many souls, who are not condemned to hell, need to be purified of the temporal punishment due for their sins. Reparation is needed to be purified for heaven. This punishment may seem severe, but only perfected souls can enter heaven in My glory. The souls in hell suffer the flames and the absence of My love forever with no hope of escaping. The souls in purgatory at least have hope that they will be released one day for heaven. The souls, who need more purification, are suffering in flames in their spirit bodies, and they do not experience My loving Presence. Those souls, who need less purification, are in upper purgatory in a grey area, but they still long to be with Me. All souls in purgatory are saved, but they require your prayers and Masses to be freed from their punishment. They cannot free themselves, or pray for themselves. In the vision you saw how a soul fell into the various levels of purgatory after that soul received its judgment. Remember to take advantage of My Divine Mercy Sunday after Easter, so you can receive a plenary indulgence that can remove all reparation due for your sins. This could lessen your time in purgatory. After seeing the suffering of these souls in purgatory, now you see how desperately they are pleading for your prayers and Masses to release them into heaven. Once these souls are freed, they will pray for you both on earth and if you will suffer in purgatory."*

Sunday, November 3, 2013:
At Holy Name after Communion I could see a very large balcony of onlookers from heaven as they watched us on the stage of life on earth. Jesus said: *"My people, in the Gospel you saw how Zacchaeus, the tax collector, met Me on the road in Jericho, when he climbed up into a sycamore tree. I told him that I wished to have supper with him that night. Once I arrived, Zacchaeus had a conversion in offering to return any money that he had cheated anyone. I commended his change of*

heart, and I gave glory that salvation came to his house that night. It is not easy for people to convert their lives from a way of sin, unless they were given a grace to do so. In the vision you see how you are actors on the stage of life. All of heaven is viewing your every action. You all are being called to follow Me, and imitate My life. It takes a great effort to lead a holy life, because you have to overcome the desires of the flesh. So when someone does convert his or her life, it is reason for celebration in heaven. Call on Me to help you with the grace of My sacraments, so you can endure all of your physical and spiritual trials. Those souls who are saved, will have their reward with Me in heaven for all eternity."

Later, at St. Joseph's Place during the rosary I could see rainbow colored beads of a rosary meant for the children to pray on. Jesus said: *"My people, it is important to teach your children the value of a good prayer life. When you are going through life, you will encounter some difficult situations. It is then that you need to call on Me in prayer to help you get through such trouble. Without praying, your crosses will be twice as hard. You also could pray a family rosary together to give the children a good example. You remember: 'The family that prays together, will stay together.' In this day and age where you are seeing many divorces and single parent households, your prayers to keep families together are needed more than ever. You could also give some advice to your children not to live together in fornication because that is a sinful lifestyle. You can give each child a rosary and a brown scapular to protect them from the temptations of the devil. The little ones are so precious to Me, and you need to protect them even in helping prevent abortion of My babies. Keep praying for the children and their souls, so they can be protected from any abuse. Parents are responsible for the souls of their children in bringing them up in the faith. The children have free will, but keep praying for their souls even after they leave your homes."*

Monday, November 4, 2013: (St. Charles Borromeo)

At St. John the Evangelist after Communion I could see the wheels of time marching on in a large watch. Jesus said: *"My people, time is one of My gifts to you, and it is an opportunity to use it to your best advantage in helping to save your soul. The worst thing that you could do, is to waste your time in frivolous ways on your own pleasures. You could use your time to help people physically, or you could pray for souls, or evangelize them. There are many good ways to use your time, but you want to avoid the sinful ways as well. It is your good deeds and prayers that store up treasure for you in heaven. Your life on earth is not that long, and your biggest goal is to work on saving your own soul by following My Commandments. You cannot count on living to tomorrow in case you could die from an accident or a heart attack. You need to have your soul pure and ready to meet Me at your judgment every day. Treat your time as precious because people with terminal illnesses as cancer are more aware of this fact. You will be held accountable for all the time that you were given in life, so work to please Me in all that you do."*

Later, at St. Theodore's tabernacle I could see the leaves falling that seemed to be a sign of some coming serious events. Jesus said: *"My people, I am showing you these leaves falling as a sign that the one world people are edging closer to some of their planned events. They have been positioning their troops and stocking up on food and ammunition in preparation for possible riots. Many of your people are just beginning to see how much more they are going to have to pay for their Health Care Insurance. Those people among the middle class workers, will be suffering more than the rich, while the poor will not pay anything, or very little. Incomes have actually declined over the last few years, so a large expense for Health Insurance will be hard to pay for. When people find it hard to see a doctor, there could be some problems. There are other issues as well with gun control and immigration that could add to the discontent in your people. The one world people will cause some incidents to incite the people in an attempt to cause a martial law which they have been planning for some time. The Warning is close and martial law will occur after this experience. My faithful need to be prepared to come to My refuges at any time when your lives may be threatened. Mandatory chips in the body will be forced under Obamacare, and this would be another sign to leave your homes for My refuges. Watch the signs around you that I have warned you about, and you can see the major events are close to happening. Trust that I will protect My people from the evil ones."*

Tuesday, November 5, 2013:

At Sacred Heart Cathedral after Communion I could see an oven for making bread. Jesus said: *"My people, you have visited several refuges that have made some kind of ovens for baking bread. Most of these ovens are heated with wood, so you will need a supply of wood for the ovens and for any wood burners for heat or stoves. To make the bread, you will need some five gallon pails of grain and a hand grinder. You will also need yeast and baking soda to make the bread rise. This will provide fresh bread that will be consumed in a short time. You also can store loaves of bread by drying the slices on a skewer in a low heat oven until all the water is removed to make it like croutons. Once the water is removed, store the bread in plastic bags, and it will no longer turn to mold. My angels will bring you the bread of Holy Communion every day to feed your soul and your body."*

Later, at St. Theodore's Adoration I could see foreign troops moving through underground tunnels as they are being placed in positions for when martial law is declared. Jesus said: *"My people, I have been giving you messages about how the one world people are planning their martial law takeover. The vision shows you the thousands of foreign troops that are being positioned to implement martial law when they cause the big event. Already you are seeing chipped individuals hearing voices to tell them how to kill people in various places. These are the false flag terrorist acts being committed to create terror and fear, as well as a plan to confiscate your guns. The other two events will be a collapse of your financial system, and a spreading of a pandemic virus by the chemtrails in the sky. These three events will set off a declared martial law. You are seeing many denials that microchip implants will be placed in people for Obamacare. These stronger denials are a sign that they will actually do it with the signing of another Executive Order that will be kept secret. The plans for the mark of the beast with mandatory chips in the body will control people like robots for those who take the chips in the body. Refuse any chips in the body, and refuse to worship the Antichrist. My Warning will come before your lives are endangered, and you can trust in Me that I will warn you when to leave your homes for My refuges."*

Wednesday, November 6, 2013:

At St. John the Evangelist after Communion I could see Jesus telling the people not to love their possessions more than Him. Jesus said: *"My people, My two Great Commandments are first to love Me with all your heart, mind, and soul, and the second is to love your neighbor as yourself. In the Gospel I was telling the people that they had to count the cost of being My disciple. In other words, I should come first in your lives over family and possessions. You live in this world, but I do not want My disciples to be of this world. The cost of My discipleship is to follow My Commandments, and use My sacraments to keep a pure soul. This means Sunday Mass and monthly Confession should be a must. If you follow My ways instead of your own ways, then you will win your reward of eternal life with Me in heaven. If you agree to this cost of obedience to Me out of love, then you will have your reward. You also need to love your neighbor and help them in their needs, with your donations of money, time, and talent. It is love that I desire of My disciples. You have a choice by your free will to either love Me or not, but the wages of defying Me in sin is death spiritually. This death could be in hell if you refuse to love Me and your neighbor. You can call on My mercy or My justice."*

Later, at St. Theodore's Adoration I could see a dark hole with water coming up in it. Jesus said: *"My people, you have seen considerable work on fracking your oil shale to provide more natural gas and oil. There have been some good yields of oil and natural gas from these new wells. This new source will help to make your country less oil dependent on other countries. There are some negatives to this process. After a surge of production, it appears the wells will be dropping off more quickly than planned. There are still complaints that water wells are being poisoned and small earthquakes are resulting from the fracking. It is hard to weigh the cons over the new oil and natural gas, but this new source of energy comes at a cost. The long term effects on the land are yet to be determined, but if the wells go dry quicker, it could leave a lot of scars on the land being used. Many areas are reluctant to risk poisoning their water wells that are important for many people's source of water. You are seeing many debates over this environmental problem. Using new techniques for finding your needed fuels, will continue to be needed as you rely on these fossil fuels."*

Thursday, November 7, 2013:

At Holy Name after Communion I could see Jesus coming to meet us with joy to protect us. Jesus said: *"My people, you can see in today's Gospel the image of Me as the Good Shepherd. I love all of My children, and I want all of you to be found in My love. I do not want to lose even one soul to the devil. It is when you stray away from Me in sin*

that I will come searching for you, as I wait patiently for you to return to My love when you seek My forgiveness. It is harder to reach souls when they blind themselves with so many of this world's distractions. Once souls lose their way without Sunday Mass and daily prayer, they become too worldly, and they lose their focus on Me, when I should be at the center of their lives. My faithful need to be My helpers in being good Christian examples to wake up other lost sheep, so they can be open to My loving care. You need to be My evangelists to help bring these sheep to their spiritual senses, and understand how they should be living without so much sin in their lives. I do not ask you to condemn anyone in judgment, but to show them the right way to live according to My Commandments of love of Me and love of neighbor. Once you can help souls to convert their lives to My love, then you will see heaven and Me rejoicing over one sinner who repents."

Later, at the Eternal Father prayer group at Holy Name Adoration I could see an aisle in a grocery store with food tossed all around and water in the aisle from a major storm. Jesus said: *"My people, I am showing you some of the destruction going on in the Philippines with a direct hit from a large powerful typhoon. Pray for the people that will die or may be hurt in this disaster. Many homes could be destroyed with 200 mph winds. With such a large storm, their economy could suffer, as they will need a lot of effort to restore what was lost. There may be some collections taken up to help them."*

I could see a lot of complaints in the latest implementation of Obamacare. Jesus said: *"My people, you have seen the poor internet showing in this new Health Plan that was only made to handle 1,100 calls at a time. Two irritations are affecting those people who are being forced under a penalty to sign up. One problem is the favoritism and unlawful waivers being given to political groups. Another is the lie that people could keep their original health plans. The high premiums for mandated high coverage will also hurt many families who may not be able to afford it. This is another example of how your government is poor at taking over private sector businesses. Pray for all the people who will have trouble getting doctors for their needs and paying for their health care."*

I could see how many people suffered power outages and downed trees from the most recent high wind storms. Jesus said: *"My people, you are finally recovering from all the damage of your most recent wind storms of over 60 mph winds. Some people had to suffer power outages of a day or two. Others had to remove and cut up some large tree limbs that came down. I have asked My people to have a year's supply of food, and fuels as wood, kerosene, and propane for heating your house. By having preparations for any power outage, you could have food, heat, and light for any emergencies."*

I could see people signing the names of people who died this year in their Book of Remembrance in church. Jesus said: *"My people, you have just celebrated All Souls Day as you remember to pray and have Masses said for your deceased loved ones who died this year. Your Book of Remembrance is a special acknowledgment of these deceased, and a thought to pray for all souls who may still be in purgatory. Your prayers and Masses can help these souls reduce their time of suffering in purgatory."*

I could see many people afflicted with cancer and other ailments as we were praying for their intentions. Jesus said: *"My people, you have seen many people suffering with various cancers. Others are suffering from blood clots, and poor knees and feet. Once people are healed, there is a great joy of relief. Not all people are healed, and some have to deal with chronic pain or a terminal illness. Keep praying for all of those who are suffering pain of any kind. Some of you have suffered in the past, so you know what this pain is, and how it is hard to bear."*

I could see souls that are in danger of being lost if they do not convert their lives of sin. Jesus said: *"My people, you can tell when people are sick physically and are in need of a doctor. It is harder to help souls who are spiritually sick in deep sin because it may not be obvious. It is hard to look at souls, but you can see their sinful actions. Try to help your relatives and friends who are leading sinful lifestyles without judging them. Encourage them to come to Mass and Confession so they can see the need for the forgiveness of their sins. Healing the spiritually sick souls is even more important than healing the body."*

I could see some people suffering from autism, allergies, and even cancers from the GMO food they are eating, and all the medications that are causing side effects. Jesus said: *"My people, you are seeing people suffering problems in their digestive tracts and allergies from eating genetically modified foods. You also are seeing infants and young children suffering autism from the many vaccines that are forced on them. Still others are suffering from the side effects and interactions of your many medications. When you manipulate food and medicines, these side effects can result in some dramatic effects on your health. Eating organic foods and using natural medicines may be better for your overall health. Pray that people will take care of what they eat and the medicines they take."*

Friday, November 8, 2013:

At St. John the Evangelist after Communion, I could see a book case with books as in a library. Jesus said: *"My people, I am showing you a library because you have both a knowledge of worldly things, and you have a knowledge of Me and the spiritual life. You have two groups of people living in the world. You have the children of the world, who lie and cheat, and you have My children of the Light, who live righteous lives according to My Will. The path for the worldly people leads to hell, but the path for My people leads to heaven. Do not give up on worldly people, but pray for them to change their sinful ways and to follow your good example. I love everyone, but if these evil ones do not convert to loving Me, then they could be lost. You all have free will, and I do not force My love on you. But those, who refuse to love Me, and refuse to seek the forgiveness of their sins, are calling down My justice on their sinful lifestyles. Keep praying for these souls to stay open to receiving Me into their hearts and lives."*

Later, at St. Theodore's tabernacle, I was amazed how the most powerful storm ever was able to hit the Philippines with a direct hit. Jesus said: *"My people, many of you are suspicious of how such a destructive storm could happen, and be directly aimed at the middle of the Philippines. The HAARP machine that is located in Alaska, has been known for its ability to enhance hurricanes and tornadoes. This machine and other microwave pulse machines are fully capable of enhancing this typhoon, and even directing its course by varying the jet streams. It would explain how a 200 mph typhoon could be formed. The one world people are trying to kill people with all of their created disasters. This storm is so destructive that it is possible that many lives will be taken, as well as many homes that will be lost. This storm comes right after a 7.2 earthquake that killed 200 people. Pray for these people to recover from such a storm. The one world people will be accountable to Me for all the people who they are killing with their death culture."*

Saturday, November 9, 2013:
(St. John Lateran Basilica Dedication)
At Mother of Sorrows Church after Communion, I could see a vision of St. John Lateran Basilica in Rome. Jesus said: *"My people, you may be familiar with the Basilica of St. John Lateran in Rome which is your Pope's Cathedral and My Church's Mother Church. I am the foundation of My Church, and My living water flows out to everyone on earth. The focus is not so much on a physical building, as it should be on Me and My people. I set up St. Peter and the apostles to organize My Church, and My Pope son and the clergy are given the authority to carry on My work of converting souls to the faith. This is the hierarchy*

of My Church, but I also call on the laity to be evangelists of souls to convert them, and come to make Me the center of their lives. I call on everyone to love Me, but not everyone is strong enough to pay the cost of My discipleship. This is why I need My people to reach out to invite people to My banquet. Those, who refuse to love Me, could be lost, but those, who love and accept Me, will be saved."

Later, at St. Theodore's tabernacle, I could look out a jet window to see some mountains from high up in the sky. Jesus said: *"My people, every time that you come aboard an airplane, you are putting your faith and trust in the airplane and the pilot, for getting you safely to your destination. In a spiritual way, you are putting your faith and trust in Me that I will guide you to your destination in heaven. I did not promise you a smooth ride. You may have to endure life's ups and downs to get through your life. You still have the assurance that you can call on Me to send you angels when you are being tested by the evil ones. I am still watching your reaction to all of your situations, so do not get angry and over-react, even when you are criticized. Put on your seat belt, and be prepared for whatever life will bring you. Be confident in Me that you will survive the ride, if you stay close to Me in prayer and obedience to My laws."*

Sunday, November 10, 2013:

At Holy Name after Communion, I could see people being persecuted for their faith in God. Jesus said: *"My people, in the first reading from Maccabees, you saw how a whole family was killed by a king because they refused to eat pork, which was against their Jewish faith. You have seen many Christians die as martyrs for not giving up their faith. Even today, Christians are being killed in Arab countries for following their faith. In America you are beginning to see more discrimination against Christians because of your atheistic society. If you wear a cross in the work place, people are harassing you. If you desire to have a Nativity scene on your own property, you will soon be harassed by atheists. You have seen prayer removed from your schools. Even prayer in your town board meetings is meeting a Supreme Court challenge. The Ten Commandments are being harassed at many public buildings. Your atheists have been able to get the ACLU to fight any display of religion in public places. Your political correctness is taking away your free speech, and your right to express religion in public. My people need to stand up to these atheists, even if it means some persecution for your faith."*

Monday, November 11, 2013: (St. Martin of Tours)

At St. Charles Church after Communion, I could see someone raking up the leaves. Jesus said: *"My people, as you rake up your leaves, think of yourself as pulling in souls when you evangelize them and pray for them. You have seen Me as a Good Shepherd gathering in My sheep. So as you gather in your leaves, think of bringing your faith to all the souls before you. You can also think of all the souls who have gone before you, and are still in purgatory. Think of these souls and pray for them, so they can come to heaven sooner with less suffering. Pray also for the souls who died in the Philippines, and for the homeless to get food and water. By caring for your neighbors, you can store up treasure in heaven."*

Later, at St. Joseph's Place, I could see people giving congratulations to a new bishop. Jesus said: *"My people, you have been praying for a new bishop for over a year for Rochester, N.Y. Now, you have Bishop Elect Salvatore Matano as an answer to your prayers. It is appropriate after your prayers are answered, to have some prayers of thanksgiving to Me for bringing you a new bishop. It is too early to say how he will interact with your priests, and if he will stop closing churches. You can keep praying that there will be a change of heart in how your diocese has been run. There is an opportunity for some good changes that should make your faithful optimistic."*

Tuesday, November 12, 2013: (St. Josaphat)

At Holy Name after Communion, I could see someone helping a neighbor to fix a fence that was broken by a fallen tree limb. Jesus said: *"My people, I came to the earth to redeem all mankind from their sins. I came also to serve and not to be served. After the Last Supper, I washed the feet of My apostles to show them that those, who wish to be leaders, need to serve the rest. You are all My creations, and I love you so much that I died for your sins. You all were created in My Image with free will that I will not deny. I do not force My people to serve Me, but I ask you to serve Me and your neighbor out of love. The devil and his angels chose not to serve Me, and as a punishment, they were cast into hell. My people also have a choice to serve Me or not. Those, who serve Me and their neighbor, will have their reward with Me in heaven for all eternity. Those, who do not serve Me, will have the same punishment in hell, just as the devil chose. This service is to love Me and love your* neighbor. *By following My Commandments and helping your neighbor with good deeds, you will be on the right path to heaven.*"

Later, at our home during the rosary, we were seeing gold flakes on people as a sign of Our Lady's presence. We also smelled a beautiful rose odor from a bottle of miraculous rose oil, and we were looking at some beautiful miracle pictures. The Blessed Mother said: *"My dear children, I was happy that you were all able to pray my rosary together, and I offered up all of your intentions to my Son, Jesus. You were given a blessing of my gold flakes that you saw on people as a sign of my presence among you. I love all of my children, and you need to use my scapular as protection against the dangers that you face every day. It is good to carry a rosary with you, and a scapular on your body. You can also use blessed salt or holy water in blessing your vehicle when you are traveling to speak. I have my mantle of protection over all of my children who pray my daily rosary. Keep close to my Son, Jesus."*

Wednesday, November 13, 2013: (St. Frances Xavier Cabrini)

At St. John the Evangelist after Communion, I could see Jesus healing the ten lepers, and how one Samaritan returned to thank Jesus for being healed. Jesus said: *"My people, you will soon be celebrating Thanksgiving Day, and you have many things to be thankful for. Your diocese has been granted a new bishop. Your spur on your foot has been healed, and your wife's knee is getting better. You have a beautiful free country, with a sunny day and fresh air to breathe. You all have been given many gifts that you may not fully appreciate. One of the ten lepers, who were healed, came back to thank Me. But just as I asked why the other nine did not come back, so I ask all of those people who received gifts, also need to thank Me. When someone does you a favor, or provides a service, you are quick to thank that person. So when your Lord takes care of you in many ways, there is even more reason for you to say a prayer of thanksgiving to Me for answering your needs."*

Later, at St. Theodore's Adoration, I could see a door open and more evil demons were coming in the door. Jesus said: *"My people, I am showing you more evil coming in with your Obamacare, spreading same sex marriage among your states, and an increase in more couples living together in fornication without marriage. Many of your people will see large increases in their health premiums because of Obamacare that is being forced upon you. This is an attempt to destroy the middle class because they will be paying the high taxes and premiums. The poor will gain more benefits with little cost, the middle class will pay more for less coverage, and the rich will have illegal waivers to avoid paying. This is all about total control which will come as mandatory chips in the body. Your government is preparing for a revolution when high taxes and premiums will cause an uproar. Even the penalties for not joining, will be punitive to your people. This evil plan could precipitate a financial bankruptcy when your Medicaid will run out of money paying for the poor. The sins of your people in fornication and homosexual acts, will compound the evil that will bring down your country. Your abortions are adding to the evil which is weighing down your country by the killing of My little ones in the womb. The punishment for all of this evil will be a takeover of your country by the one world people who will bring America into the North American Union. This is when My people will be forced to leave for My refuges. Trust in My help to protect you from all of these evil ones."*

Thursday, November 14, 2013:
At Holy Name after Communion, I could see a woman in a poor house with snow all around the house. Jesus said: *"My people, this winter scene is a sign to you of how cold the hearts of your people are, with very little love. I have told you that the Kingdom of God is among you, and that is because of My Presence among you. I am present in My Blessed Sacrament in your tabernacles, and in the people, as you are temples of the Holy Spirit. I am all loving, but there needs to be more love in your hearts for Me and your neighbors. Your society is cold because of your death culture, where there is little regard for the preciousness of life. Many of your people are more concerned with themselves and their possessions, instead of reaching out in love to help their neighbors. When you look into people's hearts for the intentions of their actions as I do, there is little love to inspire charitable sharing. You have a sinful society in great need of repentance of their sins. Until people seek the forgiveness of their sins, they will be groping in the darkness to find their way, and their hearts will be cold to My love. This is why I need to call on My faithful to evangelize souls, so they can see the Light of My Kingdom. My faithful need to be shining examples of My love, so others will seek to share My love with everyone. It is only by My love that these cold hearts can be warmed to warm hearts who will follow My ways to heaven."*

Later, at the Eternal Father prayer group at Holy Name Adoration, I could see the destruction in the Philippines from the super typhoon. Many need food, water, and shelter. Jesus said: *"My people, this typhoon in the Philippines has killed over 4,000 people and it has affected 12 million people. You are seeing a major rescue effort going on with various countries offering aid in food, water, and first aid ships. Even your churches are taking up a second collection this weekend for the relief effort for these poor people. Pray for the recovery of these people, who are suffering greatly."*

I could see some people being asked to take a chip in the body in order to obtain their Obamacare insurance. Jesus said: *"My people, I have warned you for many years that the one world people are planning to force people to take chips in the body for their health insurance. I have also told you not to take a chip in the body, because these chips will control you like a robot with voices in your head. Do not worship the Antichrist either. When they make chips in the body mandatory for your health insurance, this will be a sign to leave for My refuges. Eventually, your authorities will come to your house to enforce these chips, and if you refuse them, they will try to kill you. When you leave your home, you will be protected by an invisible shield by your guardian angel."*

I could see technicians testing the power grid, and there were some brief power outages. Jesus said: *"My people, over these last few days, there has been some power-grid testing in your North American governments with some brief power outages. Losing electricity can be severe, especially in colder weather when your heaters may not work. Be prepared with wood and kerosene so you could survive during a power outage in the winter. Have some extra fuels and heaters, along with food, water, and light sources as candles and oil lamps. You have heard the account of the five wise virgins who had extra oil for their lamps."*

I could see a major sinkhole in Florida where a house fell in. Jesus said: *"My people, in Florida you have seen several stories about large sinkholes. This comes when water is removed for drinking, and some water wells are backfilling with ocean salt water. As the land is slowly eroding, you are seeing these sinkholes form all over that can condemn a housing area for safety reasons. This latest event actually swallowed a whole house."*

I could see more violent storms and more severe earthquakes that can be caused by man-made weather machines. Jesus said: *"My people, many people are asking how these super storms are formed, and why so many severe earthquakes are happening. Microwave pulse anomalies can trigger such storms as the latest typhoons in the Pacific Ocean. The largest microwave machine is the HAARP machine in Alaska. There are many sources of these microwave pulses in various places all over the world. The HAARP machine is being used by the one world people to create chaos with huge powerful storms and large earthquakes. Their intention is to reduce the population because many people are killed in bad storms and earthquakes. This is because Satan is leading them, and he hates man."*

I could see our planned trip occurring when we will see the 21 Missions in California. Jesus said: *"My people, you will be traveling to the 21 Missions of California as a pilgrimage, and not just a vacation tour. Take some quiet time to pray at these beautiful mission churches. Each mission is unique, as they were built for the Indians by the missionaries. You will see some good history of this area when California was just being settled. See the spirit of evangelization that went on in these earlier years."*

IN MEMORY OF

Rev. John V. Rosse

Born: July 23, 1928
Ordained: June 5, 1954
Died: November 14, 2013

I could see people talking about Fr. Jack Rosse as how they remembered him since he died today. Jesus said: *"My people, it is sad when you lose a loved one, especially an old priest friend who was your pastor for 15 years. It will be difficult not to be able to attend his funeral while you are on your trip. Pray for him."*

Father Jack said: *"Hello everyone, I am as shocked as*

you are about my sudden passing from a heart attack. I guess it was fitting that I died while I was traveling, which I did a lot as you know. I had my life review as I went over all of My assignments as a priest. I will miss my many friends, but I will be praying for all of you. I will be doing a short stay in purgatory because more is expected of us priests. Please pray for me, and have some Masses offered up for my intention. I loved life, and I enjoyed all the time that I had on earth. Now, I will be helping you in a different way. I love all of you."

Saturday, November 16, 2013: (St. Gertrude)

At St. Bridget's Church, Van Nuys, California after Communion, I could see our group starting out on our pilgrimage of the 21 Missions. I could see someone blessing the bus with holy water and blessed salt for our protection. Jesus said: *"My pilgrims, you are about to leave on a beautiful pilgrimage of the twenty-one missions of California. I am showing you the need to bless your bus with holy water or blessed salt for your protection from the demons who will be attacking you. You are calling on Me to send My angels to protect you as well from any accidents or bus failures. Your people need to pray every day to guard themselves from any anger or disagreements. You all need to be good examples of My love, so be on your good behavior. Pray that all of your luggage will be found, and so no one will get ill from his or her food."*

Sunday, November 17, 2013:

At Mission de Alcala, San Diego, California after Communion, I could see the beautiful history of this mission. Jesus said: *"My people, you are just starting out on visiting the 21 Missions with a beautiful Mass. The gardens and the grounds are beautiful also. In the readings you are seeing a mention of the end times. This is your mission, to wake up My people before I return. At the end of the Church Year, you have these readings about preparing your lives for when I will bring My victory over all the evil ones. It is a good time for people to find some quiet time so they can examine their consciences to keep a pure soul in Confession. There is also a mention of a time of persecution in standing up for your faith in Me. You could even see how the Indians killed some of the missionaries. In the end times you will see an evil in the Antichrist's reign during the tribulation. It is then that you will need to come to My refuges for protection by My angels from the evil ones. Some will be martyred, while the rest of My people will be protected and fed Holy Communion by My angels. You will have food and water multiplied, as well as your shelters. You will be living a more rustic life than your comforts of today. When you are stripped of your possessions and your earthly distractions, I will be helping you to live holy lives as the saints did. Keep close to Me in your daily prayers, and keep working to improve your faith, and your trust in Me in all that you do."*

Later, at San Juan Capistrano Mission in Capistrano, California in the chapel, I could see the friars and missionaries bringing the faith to the people in earlier years. Jesus said: *"My people, you should be thankful for the hard work and dedication of the friars who persevered over many years to bring the faith to the people. Now, you are seeing fewer people coming to church on Sunday. In some areas the churches are being closed, or used as museums. In some ways America is becoming a missionary land in need of evangelization, because the spiritual hearts are growing cold to My love. I love My people, and I do not want to see any souls lost. Your people need to repent of your sins, and you need a great renewal of the faith. I am calling on My faithful to reach out and share your faith with your neighbors. Many Catholics are no longer practicing their faith, so you need to invite them to return, and re-ignite the fire of My love in their hearts. These souls need to be awakened from their spiritual slumber, and come back to My Church, and confess their sins to the priest in Confession. Without My light and grace in your soul, it will be very difficult to enter heaven. Your goal is to save as many souls as you can from going to hell, especially the souls of your own family. My faithful need to be persistent as the friars were in praying for these souls to return to Me."*

Monday, November 18, 2013:

At St. Bridget's Church, Van Nuys, California after Communion, I could see a more obvious split in the Church between the schismatic church and the Lord's faithful remnant. Jesus said: *"My people, I have been talking to you of a coming split in My Church which is very much like the first reading when the good Israelites refused to change their religious customs, even when they were threatened with death. Even in the coming days, you are going to see some clergy who will try to change your religious customs. You will see some priests changing the words of the Consecration at Mass, and I will no longer be present in their Masses. You will see more heretical teachings that will accept New Age things as Reiki and other things that are not correct according to your Catechism of the Catholic Church. When you see these heresies, you will need to go to another church. Once the schismatic church controls most of the churches, then My faithful remnant will need to have Mass underground with a faithful priest. This division in My Church is coming among you very soon. You will also start to see a stronger persecution coming from your own government against all the people who will not obey your government mandates. They will try to force heretical things upon you, that you must reject. These evil ones will threaten your lives because of your faith. At this point of severe persecution, you will need to leave for My refuges and the protection of My angels. Be prepared to stand up for your faith, even if you are criticized for not changing your beliefs. Your life may be in jeopardy for keeping close to My ways, instead of following man's ways."*

Later, at San Fernando Mission, Mission Hills, California in the chapel, I could see how the people of the world are always cheering for the movie stars. Jesus said: *"My people, your movie stars are always in your entertainment news, and they are very famous and usually rich. On the contrary, My saints should be looked up to for their holy lives, and most of them were poor in the world's eyes. The saints are your real heroes, and you could imitate their lives to bring your souls closer to Me in heaven. Many of the saints gave up their wealth, and they held the richness of My graces in My sacraments of more value than any things of the world. All of these missions have a special character that shows how important the missionaries were in bringing the faith to the people. Even as you attend many Masses, you need to pray for your priests and bishops who need your physical and spiritual help to keep faithful to their vocations. In your rosaries, call on My Blessed Mother to keep the clergy protected under her mantle of protection."*

Tuesday, November 19, 2013:

At San Buenaventura Mission at Ventura, California after Communion, I could see the quiet beauty of some flowers in the foreground, and the busy cars of the world were passing by in the background. Jesus said: *"My people, in this vision I am showing you a contrast between the quiet flowers and the busy world of cars moving back and forth. I invite My people to come to My tabernacle for a visit, so you could come in out of your busy world and take a quiet rest from all of life's distractions. If you allow the noise of the world to block out My voice, then you may forget your prayer time. You need to plan your life around Me, instead of trying to work Me in among your daily activities. Consecrate all that you do to Me and My Blessed Mother in the morning. Then we can be helping you all day long. It is your quiet time with Me, when you recollect your life's actions so you can correct your previous mistakes. If you do not take time for Me every day, then you could lose your focus on My love. I love you every moment of every day, and you can be thinking of Me all the time as well. When I am the center of your lives, you will be doing everything for Me. Loving Me and loving your neighbor should be your focus every day."*

Later, at a Courtyard Hotel room in California during Adoration, I could see a red sky. Jesus said: *"My people, when you see a red sky at the end of the day, you know that you will have good weather the next day. Yet, even though you can read the sky, you cannot read the signs of the time. Just as I told the people of My time, even now the only sign that I will give, is the sign of Jonah. This means that your country must repent of its sins, or you will see a takeover by the one world people. You need to read the signs of evil that are getting worse in the world, as the time will lead up to the Antichrist's coming to power. You are seeing same sex marriage accepted in many states. You are also seeing more couples living together in fornication without marriage. All of these evils are leading up to the Antichrist's declaration. My Warning experience will be shared by everyone, and then events will quickly lead up to the Antichrist's short reign of less than 3½ years in the tribulation. My faithful will need to heed My warning when I will warn you that it is time to take your things to My refuges. Those, who do not leave, could be martyred at their homes, or in detentions centers for not denying their faith. So read the signs of the times, and be ready to leave quickly for My refuges."*

Wednesday, November 20, 2013:

At Mission San Louis Obispo de Tolosa at San Louis Obispo, California after Communion, I could see the Vine representing Jesus and we are the branches. Jesus said: *"My people, I am showing Myself as the Vine, and you are the branches. Those, who are with Me, will survive and be saved. Those, who fall away from Me, will be detached and wither away. In the Gospel reading I gave a parable of a king, who gave one servant ten gold coins. He earned ten more, and he was give ten cities as a reward. A second servant was given five coins, and he earned five more. This servant was rewarded with five cities. A third servant was given one gold coin, but he kept it in a handkerchief, and he wasted his talent. Again I give everyone a unique set of talents, which I expect all of you to use wisely for My glory, and not just for your own gain. I have given each of you a mission, and only by your 'yes' can you carry it out. I want all of My people to use their God-given talents, and do not bury them or ignore them. By sharing your talents, both for your own needs and the needs of others, you can store up treasure in heaven for your judgment. The good servants will have their just rewards, but those, who abused their talents, will lose the little they had."*

Later, at Adoration on the bus, I could see how reverent the Jews were in handling the Ark of the Covenant that held the Ten Commandments. Jesus said: *"My people, you have seen how reverent the Jews were in protecting My Word in My Ten Commandments. Even so, there are many of My tabernacles where My people give reverence for My Blessed Sacrament. Wherever you have Adoration of My exposed Host, you should try to make an hour for Me, and even more when there is no one to take your place. You always have Me present in your tabernacles, so please come to visit Me when you can, to make up for all of those people who do not take time to come. Attending holy hours in front of My Blessed Sacrament is another way of showing Me how much you love Me. You know that I love all of you enough to die for your sins. You express your love for Me also in your prayers, and when you can come to daily Mass. You also can express your love for Me when you pray for others, even for your enemies, or those people that you do not like. You know that I am all loving, and I ask My people to try and imitate My love of everyone as well. When you reach out to everyone in love, you are like My Light of love that shines out on everyone, and I disperse the darkness of hate that comes from the demons."*

At Soledad Mission after Communion, I could see the missionaries building the missions. Then I saw dedicated people who rebuilt or refurbished the old missions. Jesus said: *"My people, after you have seen some difficult land to live on, you can appreciate how hard it was to organize and build so many missions. Not only did the missionaries try to convert the Indians to the faith, they also had to provide a means of self-support for both themselves and the Indians. They were fortunate to get grants for the buildings, but they had to have them built and provide farms for food, clothing, and heat. This was in the late 1700's and early 1800's when life was a lot harder than now. In more recent years, you have seen dedicated people in the 1900's who were willing to restore the missions to their former appearance. Now your people can appreciate the great work of St. Junipero Serra. You have missionaries all over the world, and they are worthy of your financial and prayer support. Even your parish priests need your prayers and financial help as well. Your priests are a gift to you in providing the sacraments and your spiritual leadership. There is still a need to help evangelize the children, and the Catholics that have fallen away from their faith. My people need to keep reaching out to save as many souls as you can."*

Thursday, November 21, 2013:
(Presentation of the Blessed Mother)
At the Courtyard Hotel, Fremont, Ca. after Communion, I could see the wood placed in the fireplace to represent the fire of Jesus' Sacred Heart and Mary's Immaculate Heart. Jesus said: *"My people, when you see this fire burning in the fireplace of a home, it represents the burning*

love that My Blessed Mother and I have in our hearts for love of all of you. When you see pictures of our two hearts, you see a flame burning in each of our hearts. We want to join our hearts with you, so you can be one with us. We also want to be a part of your life so we can walk with you in all that you do. Many of you have done the consecration prayers to My Blessed Mother over thirty-three days before one of her feasts. Others have had their homes enthroned to My Sacred Heart. All of your consecrations to us enable us to help you even more in accomplishing your missions. Every day when you pray your rosaries, you are not only talking to Me, but you are inviting My Blessed Mother to bring your intentions to Me. You love all of your family members and friends, and you should keep praying for their souls so you can keep them from being lost in hell. I invite you to pray also for the poor souls in purgatory. You can even invite people, who are away from Me, to come back to Me or to know Me for the first time. My Blessed Mother and I are good role models for you to follow because we lived in God's Will, while we were on the earth. Keep a picture of our two hearts in your prayer room."

Later, at the Hotel, Fremont, Ca. during Adoration, I could see someone building a fence around their property to try and protect themselves. There was also a spiritual fence that this person built around the soul, but it kept Jesus out. Jesus said: *"My people, at times people are very defensive in wanting to run their own lives without Me interfering. This can be a form of pride when souls want to be in control of their lives. Until you can give your free will over to Me so I can lead your life, it will be difficult to fulfill your mission. It is your simple obedience to My laws that I desire from each of My disciples. When you do everything out of love for Me, I can use you and give you My graces to accomplish great spiritual things. It is these spiritual blessings that will help you overcome all of life's trials that you will face. So let go of all of your earthly desires, as in fasting, so these things do not hold you back from doing My Will. Tear down all the barriers that you build around yourself, which you think will protect you. When you put your full trust in Me, you will accomplish impossible things by My grace. I will be your defense and your shield from the evil ones, and I will see to all of your earthly and spiritual needs."*

Friday, November 22, 2013: (St. Cecilia)

At the Santa Clara Mission, Santa Clara, Ca. after Communion, I could see a heart shape, and then I could see the Sacred Heart of Jesus. Jesus said: *"My people, you are seeing a heart shape in the vision which represents love. Then I showed you My Sacred Heart which is a greater representation of My personal love. This was even ultimately shown in My death on the cross for all the sins of mankind. In the readings you saw the reverence for building a Temple, and in the Gospel I also called St. Peter and My apostles to build My Church. I defended the Temple from the vendors, as you remember that I have great zeal for My house, and it consumes Me. You have seen many beautiful church buildings, but My Church is found the most in the souls of My people, both in the clergy and the laity. This is why it is important to build up My Church in bringing your family to Me, and in reaching out to convert souls to the faith. You need to encourage your families to attend Sunday Mass, pray daily, and come to Confession at least once a month. If you do not teach the faith to your children, how are they going to teach their children? Even you grandparents need to be a good example to your grandchildren, and continue building up My Church. I am depending on My prayer warriors to keep the faith strong in your families. When you love Me, you want to share My love with everyone."*

Later, on the bus during Adoration, I could see someone coming out of their Confession, and they were ready to do their penance for their sins. Jesus said: *"My people, your penance from your Confession may be a few prayers from your priest today. In former years, your penances would be much more vigorous like wearing hair shirts, or possibly more physical suffering. You could make an extra penance of fasting from something you like, as not eating desserts or sweet things for the day. Doing a bread and water fast may be more difficult. Fasting should be done with the intention of controlling your bodily desires by the desires of the soul to please Me. It is when you allow your bodily desires to perform sinful actions, that you offend Me in your sins. The more you can control your body with penances, the easier it will be to avoid the devil's temptations. Learn from your sinful mistakes, so you can avoid them in the future. Work on your frequent sins to understand how you fell into sin. You will be attacked more when you are in occasions of sin, or when you are tired and weak. By anticipating how the devil will attack you, you can be prepared to defend your soul from committing other sins. Know that I am always willing to forgive your sins, because I want to receive you into My loving arms. Do not fear, avoid, or put off Confession, but see this sacrament as a means to keep your soul clean and ready to meet Me at your judgment."*

At the hotel room in San Francisco, Ca. after Communion, I could see a couple getting married in the Church. Jesus said: *"My people, I am showing you the marriage of a man and a woman in the Church for two reasons. The first reason is that this is the proper way to be married. Living together in fornication is not a proper marriage. Living in homosexual acts is also not a proper marriage. The second reason is that this marriage is a symbol of My people as the bride and I am the Groom who protects My Church. Marriage is a promotion of the preciousness of life because the children are born into an environment of love. Protect My babies in the womb from those who want to kill them in abortion. Protect the elderly from those who want to kill them with euthanasia. Pray for peace to protect the people from being killed in your manufactured wars. Pray for all the people who are being killed by disasters, by vaccines, and by viruses. Life is truly precious, and you are all created in My Image with free will. I want all souls to love Me and come to heaven. Keep praying for all souls that could be saved from hell. Also do not forget to pray for the poor souls in purgatory. My Communion of Saints is a union of My faithful on earth, the souls in purgatory, and My souls that are saints in heaven. Your soul's life is the most important, and you need to keep your soul on the right path to heaven."*

Saturday, November 23, 2013:

At the hotel in Fremont, California after Communion, I could see Jesus as Christ the King, and then there was a lot of evil on the earth. Jesus said: *"My son, I hear your plea that your world is so evil that you are praying to Me to bring My Warning. I have told you that I will choose the time, but I do tell you often how close it is. Remember that I am Lord over all things in this world, and I only allow the evil ones to go so far. You will be seeing many disasters, and I want you to keep doing your Masses of Reparation, especially for the souls who will die that are not ready to meet Me at their judgment. When I bring My Warning to everyone, there will be many souls who will wake up and repent of their sins. Keep praying for your families, so they will not see hell in their mini-judgment. I give hope to all of you that I will be with you to protect your souls and your bodies. Do not have fear from the evil ones because I am more powerful than they are. There will be many injustices in this world, so you will be suffering a penance from your persecutions. Your suffering will be short, but your joy with Me will be greater that you can imagine for all eternity. Rejoice in the glory of your King, and your opportunity to bring souls to Me."*

Sunday, November 24, 2013: (Jesus, King of the Universe)
At Our Lady of Peace Church during Adoration at Santa Clara, Ca., I could see Jesus as a King sitting on His throne and the Blessed Mother was dressed as a queen with a crown. Jesus said: *"My people, I am showing Myself as a King and My Blessed Mother as a queen in heaven. You are giving Me praise for My Sacred Heart, and you are honoring My Blessed Mother's Immaculate Heart. We love all of you, and My Blessed Mother and I are joined as one in two hearts, and we are inviting you to be with us for all eternity. This is the last day of your trip to the 21 Missions of California, and it is ending on the 300th Anniversary of St. Junipero Serra's birthday. You have been blessed with a beautiful pilgrimage, and we want all of you to go home with a renewed strength in your faith that you can share with your friends and family at home. We are praying for your safe travel home, as My Blessed Mother will place her mantle of protection over all of you. Rejoice in the many blessings that you have received on this pilgrimage."*

Later, at Our Lady of Peace Church, Santa Clara, Ca. after Communion, I could see Jesus dying on the cross on Mount Calvary with the two thieves on either side. Jesus said: *"My people, I am showing you how much I love all of you, such that I suffered a crucifixion for the salvation of all sinners, as I died for your sins. Even as I suffered persecution from the worldly people, so My people will also suffer persecution for My Name's sake. Even though this death of Mine may appear as a defeat, yet it was My victory over sin, death, and the devil's hold on man. You heard the beautiful words of the good thief who said: 'Remember me when you come into your Kingdom'. My words to him were the words that all of you will desire: 'This day you will be with Me in paradise.' On the top of My cross there was an inscription 'This is the King of the Jews'. Not only am I King of the Jews, I am the King of the Universe, as is the title of this feast day. This is the last Sunday of the Church*

Year, and it is appropriate to talk of the end days when I will return in victory over the evil ones. All of you know the end of this story, and the evil ones lose in hell, while My faithful will be with Me in heaven."

Monday, November 25, 2013: (St. Catherine of Alexandria)

At St. Bridget's Church, Van Nuys, Ca. after Communion, I could see a stairway and a ladder to heaven. Then I saw the Lord accepting the poor in spirit. Jesus said: *"My people, in the Gospel you read of the widow placing her few coins into the Temple treasury. I remarked how she put in all that she had, while the others put in more from their surplus wealth. There are some people who are wealthy in this world's goods, but they are poor in their spiritual wealth. Also, there are some who are rich in My spiritual gifts, but they may be poor in worldly wealth. You would rather be blessed more in spiritual gifts and treasures in heaven, than in earthly things. Where your treasure lies, so lies your heart. If your treasure is in Me in My Blessed Sacrament, then your heart is with Me. If your treasure is in worldly riches, then your heart may be in your money. Those, who put worldly things before Me, could be losing their soul, if they do not change their ways. Do not put false gods before Me, because you should be putting Me first in your life. You were seeing a stairway to heaven like Jacob's ladder. You are struggling to get close to Me, so keep your focus on Me in all that you do out of love for Me and your neighbor."*

Tuesday, November 26, 2013:

At St. Bridget's Church, Van Nuys, California after Communion, I could see a large tsunami of water coming that was triggered by an earthquake. Jesus said: *"My people, I have warned you before that you will be seeing many disasters in the end times. This vision of a large tsunami is a result of a large earthquake. In previous large tsunamis, you have seen thousands of people killed, as seen in Indonesia. You will see many killed again in this coming tsunami. This is why I have asked you to include the people in all disasters that died, in the intentions of your Reparation Masses. This is because you are about to see one disaster after another. These disasters are being allowed as a punishment for the many sins of the world. Because there are not enough people praying to make up for all the sins of the world, this is why you will be seeing so many disasters. This suffering helps to make up for the reparation due for not only individual sins, but also for national sins."*

Wednesday, November 27, 2013:

At Sacred Heart Cathedral after Communion, I could see the hand writing on the wall. Jesus said: *"My people, today's first reading from Daniel 5:10-30 was about the Chaldean King who used the sacred vessels of the Temple for drinking, while he praised the gods of silver, gold, bronze, and wood. Because he did not give praise to God, the king saw a hand writing on the wall. The first word, Mene, meant God has numbered the days of the king's kingdom, and He will put an end to it. The second word, Tekel, means the king has been weighed on the scales of justice, and he was found wanting. The third word, Peres, means the king's kingdom will be divided and given to the Medes and the Persians. I have mentioned before that all of these same warnings can be applied to America. Only it will be given over to the one world people as a punishment. America's days are also numbered when you will become a part of the North American Union. Be prepared when I will call My faithful to My refuges when your lives will be in danger."*

Later, at St. Theodore's Adoration, I could see a sundial at first, and then a time line of historical events. Finally, I saw a time line of my own life with the important dates pointed out. Jesus said: *"My son, I am showing you a little of what it will be like when you have your Warning experience. You will see a time line of your life with the various important dates of your life. You will see your graduations, your marriage, and the births of your children and grandchildren. You will also see how you have grown in your faith, and when you had a change of life when you went to Medugorje. You will see things from other people's point of view, as well as My words of advice on your actions. I will then show you your mini-judgment, and where you are headed. When you are outside of your body, and outside of time, you will have a different view of life, and what should be important for you to accomplish. You will desire to repent of your sins more than your previous Confessions. All of My people will feel a sense of a needed renewal in their spiritual lives after you have your Warning experience. Some people will have a dramatic change, some will have only a small improvement, and some will have no change in their lives. Many people have improved their spiritual lives after a near death experience, when they realize how sinful they were living. Every soul that repents and converts its life, will cause joy in heaven that they were lost, and now they are found with Me in heaven."*

Thursday, November 28, 2013: (Thanksgiving Day)

At Holy Name after Communion, I could see some traditional stained glass windows in a church. Jesus said: *"My people, you have many physical and spiritual gifts to be thankful for. Those, who have jobs and family, have great blessings. Pray for those people who are unemployed, homeless, and hungry. You could even give some donations to your local food shelves to help those who need food. When you think of all of your blessings, many times you take them for granted, but other people are not as fortunate as you are. Give praise and thanks to Me for all that you have. I look out for everyone's basic needs, but people need to help themselves with what is needed, instead of just depending on handouts. The truly disabled need help, but those, who are capable, should be trying to find work and help themselves. Be thankful that you live in a free country with many opportunities to improve yourself. This may mean working at getting a good education so you can contribute to society. Many people need to work, and sometimes endure some trials in the workplace, in order to provide for their family's food, shelter, and transportation. Families need to help each other in their basic necessities. If you can afford to share money and time with your neighbors, you can store up treasure in heaven. Do not just be concerned with your own needs, but look around to help your family, friends, and neighbors. When you help others, you can even be thankful that I give you such opportunities of grace. Again be thankful to Me for all that you are experiencing in this life."*

Friday, November 29, 2013:

At St. John the Evangelist after Communion, I could see Jesus come in victory as He had His angels cast Satan, the beast of the Antichrist, and the False Prophet into hell. Jesus said: *"My people, in the Gospel I told you that the earth will pass away, but My words are forever, and they will not pass away. I have told you that I will defeat the evil ones, and My words are true. The evil ones will have a short reign of less than 3½ years. Then I will return to cast Satan, the Antichrist, the False Prophet, and all the demons and evil people into hell. All evil will be removed from the earth when My Comet of Chastisement will strike the earth. Some of My faithful will be martyred for their faith in Me, but they will become instant saints in heaven. Then I will renew the earth, and My faithful remnant will receive their reward in My Era of*

Peace. Keep your souls pure by frequent Confession so you are ready for these end days."

Later, at St. Theodore's tabernacle, I could see lava going into the sea, and the water was boiling with steam going up in the air. Jesus said: *"My people, I gave you an earlier message about how you would see a big explosion of a volcano going off. Recently, you saw Mt. Etna erupting and also a major eruption in Indonesia. I am also reminding you of the demons that come up out of hell through the volcanoes. This is another reason for an increase in evil throughout the world. Many of your people were shopping for the usual Black Friday sales after Thanksgiving. It is sad how a lot of people shop for gifts for Christmas, but very few remember that it is My birth that should be glorified, more than the gifts. These are the last days of the Church Year before Advent starts on Sunday. There has been a lot of focus on the end days of My victory over evil. Keep focused on your final destination in heaven, more than on your possessions of this life."*

Saturday, November 30, 2013: (St. Andrew)

At Mother of Sorrows Church after Communion, I could see the apostles going out two by two to evangelize the people. Jesus said: *"My son, this feast day of My apostle, St. Andrew, is a celebration for all of My faithful who spread My Word to the people. I had to rely on My apostles and deacons to spread the Word of My Kingdom to all the nations. I am your Redeemer for your sins, and I bring salvation to all sinners through My death on the cross, and My sacraments. Those,*

who are blessed with a gift of faith, need to share their gifts to convert sinners, and bring them to the faith in Me. The people need to hear My Word, and accept it with repentance of their sins, so they can be saved in heaven. My son, you are blessed to receive My messages, which need to be revealed to My people, so they can prepare their souls for the end times. Go forth like My apostles did, to spread My Word of hope and love, so all peoples may have the opportunity to have faith in Me, and be saved from hell. I want all souls to come to Me of their own free will. Repent of your sins now while you still have time before you die."

Later, at St. Theodore's tabernacle, I could see comets in the sky that were signs of things to come. Jesus said: *"My people, you are ending the Church Year, and you will be starting your First Sunday of Advent. Even now you are seeing signs in the sky from the Ison Comet that some major events are about to start. Your scientists are forecasting many comets that will come in 2014. As these comets come closer, you may see even more unusual events in the sky. On the day of the Warning, there will be a comet going by that could be a frightening event for some people. Keep watching the skies for any signs of the major events that will lead up to the Warning and the tribulation.*"

Sunday, December 1, 2013: (First Sunday of Advent)

At Holy Name after Communion, I could see the coming of Jesus, but it was at the end times. Jesus said: *"My people, the Gospels of the last Sunday of the Year and the first Sunday of the Church Year are similar in that they speak of My glorious victory when I will return. There is mention today of My coming, but the real focus should be on My victory, rather than on My being honored at Christmas. I already came to the earth once to die for mankind's sins, but My next coming will be to separate the evil ones from My faithful. You do not know when this Chastisement will come, nor do you know when I will come for you at your death. In either case, you need to be watchful, and ready with a pure soul by frequent Confession. Many people are unprepared for their judgment because I will truly come when you least expect Me. This is the point of today's Gospel in that you need to be ready to meet Me at your judgment every day. Then you will be like the wise virgins, and not like the foolish virgins who were unprepared when the bridegroom came.*"

Monday, December 2, 2013:

At St. John the Evangelist after Communion, I could see the deep faith of the Roman centurion. Jesus said: *"My people, I had healed many people on the earth, and those, who were healed, needed to have faith that I could heal them. The Roman centurion's faith was remarkable, considering that he was not even a Jew. He recognized My healing power, and he believed that I could heal his paralyzed servant, even from a distance. He knew that Jews would be defiled to enter the centurion's house, so he said the words that you repeat at the Communion time: 'Lord, I am not worthy that you should enter under my roof, but only say the word, and my soul shall be healed.' I acknowledged the centurion's faith by claiming that I did not see such faith in all of Israel. In the same way, I desire that all of My people should have this strong faith in Me for healing all of their ailments. Ask and you shall receive, knock, and the door will be opened to you."*

Later, at St. Theodore's tabernacle, I could see some large icebergs break off in Antarctica that could be dangerous for shipping. Jesus said: *"My people, you are aware of the history of the Titanic in how it struck an iceberg and it sank. This vision of icebergs forming, is a sign to you of how America could easily be like the Titanic. You are seeing how a major incident will be perpetrated to cause a major event that could kill a lot of people, and it could be an excuse for martial law and the potential downfall of your country. You are seeing signs of your government preparing for something big, because they are ordering a lot of ammunition and food. This means that what is coming, has been planned, and it might involve the HAARP machine. I have told you that when your life is endangered, or you see a national martial law declared, that you will need to flee to My refuges. It is part of the one world people's plan to reduce the population, so do not be surprised at the scope of a large event that could kill a lot of people. Have your soul prepared by frequent Confession, and have your bags packed and ready to flee to My refuges."*

Tuesday, December 3, 2013: (St. Francis Xavier)

At Holy Name after Communion, I could see a priest giving a homily from a raised podium. Jesus said: *"My people, the Catholic faith needs the underpinnings of a good prayer life, Sunday Mass, and frequent Confession. There is also another element, and that is developing a true loving, personal relationship with your Lord. Do not just repeat words in your prayers, but you need to pray from the heart. When you keep telling Me how much you love Me, I should be able to see your sincerity in how you love Me and your neighbor. You need to reach out with acts of charity in helping your family, and your neighbors both with your money and your time. The more you do out of love for Me, the more treasure you will store up in heaven for your judgment. The most important sharing of all is when people see how your love for Me has inspired your life. Then they will desire My love as well. Remember to make love and concern for each other a daily focus by calling on My grace, and keeping your focus on Me in your life. Those, who seek Me out of love and obedience, will have their reward in heaven."*

Later, at St. Theodore's Adoration, I could see a general decline in Church attendance on Sunday, and the collections have dropped. Jesus said: *"My people, you are seeing the possibility of more churches closing, not only due to a priest shortage, but fewer people are attending Sunday Mass. As your numbers drop, the collections are going down as well. Even the uncertainty of a church closing, is causing your numbers to go down as well. You have a new bishop in your diocese, so it is hard to know what he will do to address this problem. Keep praying to keep your churches open, or you could lose even more members who will not go to another church. In the same way, you need to pray for your priests, and for more vocations to the priesthood. You should treasure even your retired priests who are providing for your Masses. Without enough priests, you could also find it hard to have Confession times available. The sign of the faith getting weaker among your people, is another sign that you are in the end times where evil is getting stronger. I am more powerful than the demons, but My faithful need to keep close to Me for their protection."*

Wednesday, December 4, 2013: (St. John Damascene)
At St. John the Evangelist after Communion, I could see the priest raising the Host at the Consecration. Jesus said: *"My people, the Gospel is a sign of My Eucharist in the multiplication of the bread and the fish for the 4,000. I love all of you enough to die for your sins, but I also left you My Eucharistic Real Presence, so I could always be with you. You need bread to nourish the body, but you also need My Eucharistic Bread to nourish your soul with My grace. I am the Bread of life, but*

there are some who do not believe in My Real Presence. This miracle of My transubstantiation from bread into My Body and Blood, is a gift that only My true believers can understand by their faith in Me. It is truly an act of faith that is required, because this teaching of My Church is a mystery to understand. Yet, I am present in all of your tabernacles, where you can come and visit your Lord. Give thanks to Me for this sacrament, and all of My sacraments. When you receive Me worthily, I come into your soul to grant you My grace, and I share My love with you intimately. Rejoice to be with Me at every Mass that you can attend."

Later, at St. Theodore's Adoration, I could see many people putting up their Christmas decorations for both inside and outside. Jesus said: *"My people, in many homes you see an array of lights, Santa Claus, snowmen, and reindeer. It is unusual to see outside Nativity displays as you have. There are even some places that try to ban any outside Nativity scenes, even on your own property. It is the atheists who are trying to take all public displays about Me out of public places. My people need to stand up against these atheists for all of their political correctness. You would rather please Me, more than mankind. You are seeing attacks against Me when people are criticized for wearing crosses, when the Ten Commandments are removed from public buildings, and when prayer is removed from the schools. This is just the beginning of the coming persecution of Christians. When you are tested, defend your faith in Me, and do not deny Me, even if the authorities threaten to kill you. Do not take any flu shots, or chips in the body. When your lives are threatened, you will have to leave for My refuges while you are guarded by your guardian angels. Those, who are true to Me in their persecution, will have their reward in My Era of Peace, and later in heaven."*

Thursday, December 5, 2013:

At Holy Name after Communion, I could see Jesus giving His Sermon on the Mount. Jesus said: *"My people, today's Gospel offers you an obvious choice of your free will that I do not force on you. You can believe in Me, and have faith in My Word, and you will be like the man who built his house on rock. I built My Church on the Rock of St. Peter, and I have been true to My Word in not allowing the gates of hell to prevail over it. You can also refuse My love and refuse to accept*

Me, but this will have consequences, as the man who built his house on sand, and the winds and rain brought it to ruin. In every action you perform, there is a decision for Me, or against Me. You cannot just say Lord, Lord, and you will be saved. I need to see by your good deeds in your actions that you truly believe, and you are acting out your faith in Me in your everyday actions. This will be your affirmation of your love for Me, that you do not want to offend Me by your sins. At times you may fall in human weakness, but you can return to My grace in Confession. At your judgment you will be held accountable for all of your actions. I love the sinner, but not his or her sinful actions. You all are good persons, as I created you, but it is your actions that will determine your eternal destination."

Later, at the Eternal Father prayer group at Holy Name Adoration, I could see a great white Light of Jesus as He listened to our prayer requests. Jesus said: *"My people, you are praying to keep your church open and viable. There is still a chance that your church could be closed, but it could be clustered just as well. You were graced with a pastor for a while, but now it appears unlikely to have another priest. Keep praying that your new bishop will not close your church, and possibly he could bring in some priests from outside of your diocese."*

I could see good neighbors who help each other, especially in weather problems. Jesus said: *"My son, I am happy that you were able to repair your neighbor's fence, even amidst a few difficulties. This shows that when you are sincere in trying to correct a tree falling on a fence from a storm, that you can find a way to make it work. Your neighbor is probably happy that you could fix it, and remove the tree without much expense. You are a good example to others that you reached out to help your neighbor."*

I could see continuing problems with people losing their health insurance. Jesus said: *"My people, you are seeing a continuation of problems with your Obamacare. Even people who could get signed up, may find it hard to connect with paying their premiums to the insurance companies. Higher charges are hurting people's budgets who cannot afford these increases. Getting younger people to sign up, is not happening soon enough to pay for those new people who are not paying much. Pray that these new taxes do not destroy your economy."*

I could see many hidden flaws in the Health Care Law that could threaten people with chips. Jesus said: *"My people, it is the hidden parts of your Health Care Law that could present more threats to your lives, and not just higher insurance costs. There was an original intention in this law to control people by forcing you to have mandatory chips in the body. Do not take any chips in the body, no matter how much your authorities want to threaten you. These chips will control your minds with voices, and they will make you like robots. When you see mandatory chips in the body, this will be a time to leave for My refuges, because the evil ones will threaten to kill you for not going along with their new world order. This mark of the beast is at the door, as this Obamacare Law is about to be fully implemented."*

I could see people preparing for Christmas, as they are buying gifts for their friends and family. Jesus said: *"My people, I understand how you all love to share gifts with each other for Christmas. Do not get so taken up with your shopping that you forget to honor My birthday as the central theme of Advent. I came as your Savior to redeem all of you from your sins. Think of Advent as a smaller Lent when you take time to recollect your sins, and try to improve your spiritual lives. Try to get to Confession before Christmas, so you can present your pure soul to Me as your gift."*

I could see two big feast days of the Blessed Mother coming with the Immaculate Conception and Our Lady of Guadalupe. Jesus said: *"My people, I know that you love My Blessed Mother, and she loves all of you as well. Honor her on her feast days by coming to Mass on these days. My Blessed Mother is a central figure in Christmas because she bore Me in her womb for nine months. Give thanks for her 'yes' and thank her for looking over her children with her mantle of protection."*

I could see the beauty of God's love in His desire to become a man so He could die for our sins. Jesus said: *"My people, you are aware of My Blessed Mother's 'yes' to be My mother, but I also had to give My 'yes' to become a man to carry out My Father's plan of salvation for all of mankind. I had two moments of testing in the Garden of Gethsemane and before I died on the cross. In essence, I told My Father that it was not My Will, but His Will that needed to be done. This is the same for all of My faithful souls. You need to give up this life, and give your will over to Me, in order to be saved. Once you appreciate the beautiful reward that awaits you in heaven, any suffering on earth would be well worth such a reward. I love all of you, and I strive to win every soul."*

Friday, December 6, 2013: (St. Nicholas)

At St. John the Evangelist after Communion, I could see the two blind people suffering without their sight. Jesus said: *"My people, as you go through this life, you may be called to suffer in many different ways because of your fragile body that you have in this mortal life. When you are well, you can accomplish many things, but when you are sick or injured, you will be suffering to do everyday chores. Sometimes I test you with sickness to keep you humble. Even when you are sick or hurting, you can call on My help, as the blind people did, and you can offer up your suffering for sinners and the souls in purgatory. No matter what your earthly body causes you to suffer, still keep your focus on loving Me, and do not despair of any difficulties. It may be easy to get discouraged when things are not going your way, but do not let earthly problems take you away from your focus on Me. I do help heal people with earthly trials, but struggle along the best that you can with your own physical hurts. I see all that you are suffering, and you will be rewarded in heaven."*

Saturday, December 7, 2013: (St. Ambrose)

At Mother of Sorrows Church after Communion, I saw the supports and underpinnings of a bridge, meaning a person's faith has to be well grounded in the truths of the faith. Jesus said: *"My people, a good Christian needs to have a good foundation in the teachings of My Church. I told you before how you need to build your house on rock so when the winds of adversity of the world come, you can withstand this trial because you had a firm foundation. How does one build such a firm foundation? You need to study and know your Catechism of the Catholic Church. Read or pray the Apostle's Creed, and you will have the basics of the faith. Some were taught the faith in a Catholic grammar school, high school, or college. Others have been trained in your RCIA program as they were brought into My Church by Baptism, Holy Communion, and Confirmation. My sacraments are instrumental in maintaining your faith, especially in Confession and Holy Communion. Your prayer life is another building block to support your faith and love for Me. By obeying My Commandments and loving your neighbor, you can be on the right path to heaven. Being with Me in heaven should be your goal throughout your whole life. I love all of you so much, and I want you to show Me your love every day. I died for your sins to show you how much I love you. That is why the big crucifix on the altar should remind you of My love every time you look at it. You can show Me your love in your daily prayers and good deeds. Once you have a good foundation in the faith, you need to build on it, by working to improve your spiritual life every year on a steady path to perfection. I will help support you on your way to becoming a saint with Me in heaven. Sainthood is the ultimate crown for a soul on earth, and do not allow the evil ones to detour you from this path."*

Later, at St. Theodore's tabernacle, I could see a woman looking out into a world of war from inside a car window. Jesus said: *"My people, the Bible speaks of how the wages of sins are death. If you were able to look around at all of your households as I do, you would see all the sins of fornication, homosexual sin, prostitution, abortion, and birth control. This is rampant all over the world, as these sins are causing many killings in wars. Many of your family oriented traditions have become invaded by the worldly pleasures of life. Your movies and magazines flaunt living together without marriage as a norm for your society. Your people are more interested in their bodily pleasures, than in loving Me and following My Commandments. Living the restrictions of a proper married life have been cast aside by those who have lost their morals of a right conscience. Many young people know it is a mortal sin to have sex outside of marriage, but they have blinded their minds with bodily lust. These sinners will be held accountable for their sins, and they need prayers to repent, and change their lifestyle. You all have read about Sodom and Gomorrah, and how they were destroyed because of their sexual sins. America and many other countries will be paying the price of their sins when I bring many disasters and one world control over all the nations. Repent now while you can still save your souls."*

Sunday, December 8, 2013:

At Holy Name after Communion, I could hear the reading of Isaiah that spoke of the 'Stump of Jesse'. Jesus said: *"My people, this reference of Isaiah to the stump of Jesse is to the father of King David. Both My parents were also descendants of King David, which is why some people called Me the 'Son of David'. I call your attention today to generational healing because this is so linked to the 'human' weakness of sin that your priest spoke of in his homily. In some families there is a tendency to a weakness to drinking in excess. In other families it is a weakness to gambling. Many families also have a lust for sexual pleasure without marriage in living together. These sins can be rooted in generational sins that get passed on to the children. Generational healing starts with an exorcism of the family members so this inherited weakness of a particular sin from a demon can be rooted out from this family. It also involves praying for the family every day, so the members who are weaker, can be brought back to Me in Sunday Mass, and repentance of their sins in Confession. My arms are always open to receive all sinners if they would just listen to the words of St. John the Baptist when he said: 'Repent and be saved.' Family members need to see that I am missing in their lives, and they need to wake up to My love that calls them to Me. The best deliverance prayers are to pray the long version of the St. Michael prayer over the pictures of the family, and place some blessed salt or holy water on the pictures. Repeat this as many times as you can in the coming days, and do not give up on any sinner because I do not."*

For those who do not know the long form of the St. Michael prayer, here it is: (An exorcism prayer) (+) Use the sign of Cross

Prayer to St. Michael the Archangel: In the Name of the Father, and of the Son, and of the Holy Ghost. Amen.

Most glorious Prince of the Heavenly Armies, Saint Michael the Archangel, defend us in "our battle against principalities and powers, against the rulers of this world of darkness, against the spirits of wickedness in the high places'. (Eph. 6:12)

St. Michael the Archangel, Defend us in the Battle.

Come to the assistance of men whom God had created to His likeness and whom He has redeemed at a great price from the tyranny of the devil. The Holy Church venerates you as her guardian and protector; to you, the Lord has entrusted the souls of the redeemed to be led into heaven. Pray therefore the God of Peace to crush Satan beneath our feet, that he may no longer retain men captive and do injury to the Church. Offer our prayers to the Most High, that without delay they may draw His mercy down upon us; take hold of "the dragon, the old serpent, which is the devil and Satan," bind him and cast him into the bottomless pit "that he may no longer seduce the nations". (Rev. 20:2-3)

Exorcism:

In the Name of Jesus Christ, our God and Lord, strengthened by the intercession of the Immaculate Virgin Mary, Mother of God, of Blessed Michael the Archangel, of the Blessed Apostles Peter and Paul and all the Saints that are powerful in the holy authority of our ministry, we confidently undertake to repulse the attacks and deceits of the devil. God arises; His enemies are scattered and those who hate Him flee before Him. As smoke is driven away, so are they driven; as wax melts before the fire, so the wicked perish at the presence of God.

V. Behold the Cross of the Lord, flee bands of enemies

R. The Lion of the tribe of Judah, the offspring of David hath conquered.

V. May Thy mercy, Lord, descend upon us.

R. As great as our hope in Thee.

We drive you from us, whoever you may be, unclean spirits, all satanic powers, all infernal invaders, all wicked legions, assemblies and sects.

In the Name and by the power of Our Lord Jesus Christ, + may you be snatched away and driven from the Church of God and from the souls made to the image and likeness of God and redeemed by the Precious Blood of the Divine Lamb.

+ Most cunning serpent, you shall no more dare to deceive the human race, persecute the Church, torment God's elect and sift them as wheat.

+ The Most High God commands you, + He with whom, in your great insolence, you still claim to be equal.

"God who wants all men to be saved and to come to the knowledge of the truth." (1 Tim 2:4)

God the Father commands you. + God the Son commands you. + God the Holy Ghost commands you.

+ Christ, God's Word made flesh, commands you; + He who to save our race outdone through your envy, "humbled Himself, becoming obedient even unto death" (Phil. 2:8); He who has built His Church on the firm rock and declared that the gates of hell shall not prevail against Her, because He will dwell with Her "all days even to the end of the world." (Mt. 28:20)

The Sacred Sign of the Cross commands you, + as does also the power of the mysteries of the Christian Faith.

+ The glorious Mother of God, the Virgin Mary, commands you; + she who by her humility and from the first moment of her Immaculate Conception crushed your proud head.

The faith of the holy Apostles Peter and Paul, and of the other Apostles commands you. + The blood of the Martyrs and the pious intercession of all the Saints commands you. +

Thus cursed dragon, and you, diabolical legions, we adjure you by the living God, + by the true God, + by the holy God, + by the God "who so loved the world that he gave up His only Son, that every soul believing in Him might not perish but have life everlasting" (Jn 3:16) stop deceiving human creatures and pouring out to them the poison of eternal damnation; stop harming the Church and hindering her liberty.

Begone, Satan, inventor and master of all deceit, enemy of man's salvation. Give place to Christ in Whom you have found none of your works; give place to the One, Holy, Catholic and Apostolic Church acquired by Christ at the price of His Blood. Stoop beneath the all-powerful Hand of God; tremble and flee when we invoke the Holy and terrible Name of Jesus, this Name which causes hell to tremble, this Name to which the Virtues, Powers and Dominations of heaven are humbly submissive, this Name which the Cherubim and Seraphim praise unceasingly repeating: Holy, Holy, Holy is the Lord, the God of Hosts.

V. O Lord, hear my prayer.
R. And let my cry come unto Thee.
V. May the Lord be with Thee.
R. And with thy spirit. Let us pray.

God of heaven, God of earth, God of Angels, God of Archangels, God of Patriarchs, God of Prophets, God of Apostles, God of Martyrs, God of Confessors, God of Virgins, God who has power to give life after death and rest after work: because there is no other God than Thee and there can be no other, for Thou art the Creator of all things, visible and invisible, of Whose reign there shall be no end, we humbly prostrate ourselves before Thy glorious Majesty and we beseech Thee to deliver us by Thy power from all the tyranny of the infernal spirits, from their snares, their lies and their furious wickedness. Deign, O Lord, to grant us Thy powerful protection and to keep us safe and sound. We beseech Thee through Jesus Christ Our Lord. Amen.

V. From the snares of the devil,
R. Deliver us, O Lord.
V. That Thy Church may serve Thee in peace and liberty:
R. We beseech Thee to hear us.
V. That Thou may crush down all enemies of Thy Church:
R. We beseech Thee to hear us.

(Holy water or blessed salt is sprinkled on the pictures.)

St. Michael the Archangel defend us in battle. Be our protection against the wickedness and snares of the devil. May God rebuke him, we humbly pray, and do thou, O Prince of the heavenly hosts, by the Divine power of God, thrust into hell Satan, and all the other evil spirits who prowl about the world seeking the ruin of souls. Amen.

Monday, December 9, 2013: (Immaculate Conception)

At St. John the Evangelist after Communion, I could see a gold crown over the Blessed Mother in heaven, as giving her 'yes' to the Angel Gabriel was a crowning touch of her part in our salvation. Jesus said: *"My people, ever since Adam and Eve sinned, and were driven out of the Garden of Eden, I promised man that I would send a Redeemer to give hope to all souls. Until I died, no soul was able to come to heaven, so the righteous souls had to suffer not seeing Me. From this time I also have prepared My Blessed Mother so she would be a sinless woman to conceive Me in her immaculately conceived soul. My Blessed Mother would become the new Eve for all of her children. This feast is celebrated on Monday because of the Second Sunday of Advent which was on December 8th. At the Annunciation this was My Blessed Mother's finest hour when she gave her free will 'yes' to My Archangel Gabriel to be My mother. This is when, by the power of the Holy Spirit, I was conceived in her womb. This began the sequence of events that would allow My Incarnation as a man that would lead to mankind's redemption by My death on the cross. Rejoice in My Blessed Mother's acceptance of her mission as the Mother of God. Rejoice also in her title as the Immaculate Conception which is honored as America's patroness in Washington, D.C."*

Later, at St. Theodore's tabernacle, I could see a lot of snow and ice disasters. Jesus said: *"My people, you are seeing many power outages and flight cancellations, due to two major snow and ice storms that have spread across your country. This caused school closings, accidents, and some deaths. I told you that because of your many sins, you would be seeing one disaster after another. Now, you are seeing these things brought right before your eyes. Many of these storms have happened before at this time, but you are seeing record cold and heavy snow in places that do not have such severe weather. Be prepared to endure more of these storms, as your weather patterns and jet streams are becoming more erratic and unpredictable. Some news people noted a possible effect on Christmas shopping, but ice damage has affected power lines and car damage. Some predictions of a bad winter are already in your headlines. This is another example why it would be helpful to have some extra food and alternative fuels for any power outages. Some extra lamp oil would help to provide light when the power is off. It is good to be prepared for both physical and spiritual hard times."*

Tuesday, December 10, 2013:

At Holy Name after Communion, I could see Jesus leaving the ninety-nine sheep in the desert, as He went out to look for the lost sheep. Jesus said: *"My people, I have told you many times that I do not want to lose any soul. Because so many Christians have fallen away from their faith, now, I am searching for more than one sheep. There are more sheep who are lost, than the few sheep who are still coming to Sunday Mass. I wait for the return of My lost sheep, but it is even better if I send My faithful out to bring in the lost sheep. I have told you the story of the Prodigal Son, and how he finally returned because he was hungry, and in search of My forgiveness. I do not force My love on people, but I want you to love Me of your own free will. Those, who love Me, are so happy and filled with My love, that they want to share My love*

with everyone. *Once souls return to seek My forgiveness, I will forgive them, and I will receive them with love and joy because they were lost, and now they are found. All of heaven rejoices over every sinner who repents and is converted from any sinful ways."*

Later, at our home we were watching our Adoration DVD because of a snowstorm, I could see a brick wall falling apart. Then I could see a double helix that referred to a manipulation of DNA as with GMO. Jesus said: *"My people, you are familiar with the Isaiah 9:10 prophecy that starts with the bricks have fallen. This vision is suggesting that the Harbingers are a warning for America, that if you do not repent as a nation, then you will be brought to your knees by the one world people. I have given you many messages of how your nation will fall under martial law, and My faithful will need to seek My protection at*

My refuges. The vision of the DNA refers to how your seed companies have manipulated the DNA of your crops to make GMO crops that are causing allergies and cancers. This manipulation and control of the food is why you will see a man-made controlled famine. I also have had My faithful store some non-GMO or heirloom seeds, so you can grow crops as I made them without causing any disease. I will need to renew the whole earth after the tribulation because of how man has abused My creation. You will rejoice when I will bring you into My Era of Peace as your reward for all that you will suffer. Do not have any fear of the end times because I will give you a peace about all of these events. Have no fear of the evil ones because My angels will protect you."

Wednesday, December 11, 2013: (St. John of Damascene)
At St. John the Evangelist after Holy Communion, I could see a heavenly Light of God over the earth as a blessing. Jesus said: *"My people, I am the Light of the world, and I disperse the darkness of sin, as I comfort My people. I call My people to comfort them, for My yoke is easy and My burden of faith is light. Advent is a time of joy and preparation for My coming at Christmas. Even though you are suffering from the cold and the snow of winter, it does cover everything with a white coating over the drab landscape without green leaves. You are buying gifts for your loved ones, so you can share your Christmas joy with them. It is also nice to share some financial help with your friends and relatives as well. The best gift that you could give your loved ones is some prayers, even for deliverance of any addictions. Keep praying for your family members, for you could be the salvation of their souls."*

Later, at St. Theodore's Adoration, I could see people living in a rustic setting. Jesus said: *"My people, when it comes time to leave for My refuges, it will be hard to provide for your food, heating, and shelter. During the winter, it will be harsh to deal with the cold. If you have a steady supply of natural gas from the ground, you could keep warm. If you have wooded land, you could chop up logs for firewood. I will multiply your fuels for heating and cooking. People, who have chickens, can have eggs, but you need a multiplied source of chicken feed. I will send deer to your camps for meat, but you need hunters to cut up and handle the meat. You will need various skills to provide for yourselves. You will have angels to protect you, and they will bring you daily Communion. You will be praying more at Adoration at each refuge.*

You will have water and a luminous cross to heal your ailments. You can keep your food in a root cellar in the ground. You will need to provide latrines for the people's needs. During the summer, you could farm some crops with your heirloom seeds. Once you are used to providing for food and heat, then you will only see these chores as a way of life, that is much simpler than how you are living in your modern comforts. You can adapt to a rustic life because that will be the only way to live with My help and My angel support."

Thursday, December 12, 2013: (Our Lady of Guadalupe)
At Holy Name after Holy Communion, I could see Our Lady dressed in the sun. The Blessed Mother said: *"My dear children, this miraculous image of myself as pregnant with my Son, Jesus, is an image that makes*

me the Mother of the Americas. This image is a support for all pregnant mothers, and I support life in all of its stages. Earlier, it was a sign for the Indians to stop offering up their infants to the gods. Today, this image is dedicated to stopping all abortions where you give up your infants to the gods of pleasure, riches, and convenience. I have been behind Right to Life movements all along. This image of Juan Diego also is a sign out of the Book of Revelation as the woman dressed in the sun as in your vision. This image is a sign of the end times that my Son has asked you to get the people prepared for. I am the refuge of sinners, and my Son wants His people to be protected at His physical refuges during the coming tribulation. Remember that I am protecting all of my children with my mantle of protection."

Later, at the Eternal Father prayer group at Holy Name Adoration, I could see a lot of snow and cold descending on the northern part of America. Jesus said: *"My people, your people have been suffering from a large cold wave that has come down from Canada. Many of your people have endured heavy snow and ice storms that have caused several power outages. Each year, you expect this in winter, but it does seem a little more severe and colder than usual. These snow disasters are just a taste of what is to come. Keep praying to counter all the sin in your country. This extra coldness is another sign of the love that is lacking both for Me and for your fellow citizens."*

I could see some peace signs among the Congress people. Jesus said: *"My people, your Congress has finally reached an accord in dealing with your budgets and taxes. With passage in the Senate, then your Congress people can start managing their budgets with the proper appropriations for each department of your government as you used to do. This will put more focus on how to fix your Health Care law that appears to be having problems for people to sign up, and to pay for their health insurance premiums. Many are seeing that they cannot afford to pay for a one-size-fits-all insurance with high premiums and high deductibles. Pray for some fair payments so the middle class does not have to shoulder most of this burden."*

I could see people buying gifts for their family members. Jesus said: *"My people, it is good to share your gifts, but I gave you an even better suggestion to pray your deliverance prayers for the souls of your family members. I had you give the people the long St. Michael prayer* (Dec. 8, 2013 message) *so they could pray over the pictures of their family members. These prayers are needed to atone for their sins, and to help open their hearts and souls to My love. I asked you to pray these deliverance prayers often for the intentions of your family that have strayed away from Me."*

I could see the days drawing closer to Christmas. Jesus said: *"My people, this Sunday you will already be celebrating the Third Sunday of Advent with a pink candle and vestments. This season is very short, so spend some time in prayer as you prepare your gifts for Me at My crib. You prepare gifts for your family and friends, so you should think to offer Me a personal gift as well. Even if you make an attempt to get to Confession before Christmas, this would be a great gift to Me, and it will benefit your soul also."*

I could see many families who try to get together to share a Christmas meal and gifts. Jesus said: *"My people, not all families are on good speaking terms with each other. Christmas should be a time of joy, so families can patch up their differences, and move on with their lives. Life is too short to hold grudges, and be constantly fighting. It is time to have peace in all families, so I can come into all of your hearts to share My peace and love."*

At times I can see more people coming to Christmas Mass than at other times of the year. Jesus said: *"My people, I am happy to see so many new faces that make an effort to see Me at My crib at Christmas Mass. I pray that these same people would make more of an effort to come to Mass on the other Sundays of the year. I am always present at the Consecration of the Mass, not only on Christmas, but at every Mass. It is well to receive Me in Holy Communion worthily as often as you can. If you truly love Me, you could show Me more than once a year, or once a week. I love all of you every day, so tell Me of your love for Me in your daily prayers."*

I could see that many people are familiar with today's feast day of Our Lady of Guadalupe. Jesus said: *"My people, I want you to help celebrate My Blessed Mother's feast day by praying for the stoppage of abortion. Your country will pay a heavy price for all the babies that you kill in America every year. Think of My Blessed Mother's image of a pregnant woman, and see the need to try and encourage your mothers not to have any more abortions. Each conceived child has a plan for his or her life, and if you kill that life, then you are blocking My plan for that child. You will have to make amends for any killing, and for the loss of the plan that could have helped your society. Rejoice in My Blessed Mother's feast and tell her how much you love her."*

Friday, December 13, 2013: (St. Lucy)

At St. John the Evangelist after Holy Communion, I could see some poor people who needed a glass of water. Jesus said: *"My people, most of your people in America have the basic necessities to survive in at least an apartment in the winter. People, who do not work for a living, have access to welfare and food stamps. Some poor people are not well educated, and these are the ones who call on your local food shelves to get by. Sometimes your social workers have to help the poor to fill out forms to get what aid is available. This aid can vary from state to state. As you see this vision of someone requesting a glass of water, you need to share what you can with your local poor with donations to your food shelves. Have mercy on those people who are less fortunate, as they need the basics of food and shelter. All of your help will be stored up in heaven for your judgment. When you look at a poor person, you are seeing Me in them making a request for help."*

Later, at St. Theodore's tabernacle, I could see a fault line in the earth as it widened to the coastline, and water filled in the crack. Jesus said: *"My people, the earthquake that you are seeing, is how the New Madrid fault will open up all the way to the Gulf of Mexico, and the ocean will fill in the fault. When you see a major earthquake along the New Madrid fault, you could see some major changes in the geography of the Mississippi Valley. Such a quake could kill thousands of people, and destroy many homes. This event could well trigger a martial law with a huge effect on your country's economy. I have been warning you of possible large quakes both in California and along the New Madrid fault, that could be caused by the HAARP machine. Pray for the souls who could die in such a quake, when they may not be ready to meet Me at their judgment."*

Saturday, December 14, 2013: (St. John of the Cross)

At Sacred Heart Cathedral after Holy Communion, I could see Elijah with Jesus on Mt. Tabor. Jesus said: *"My people, you remember the account of My Transfiguration on Mt. Tabor, when I appeared in My glorified Body as a preview of My Resurrection. Elijah and Moses appeared with Me before My apostles Peter, James, and John. Peter wanted to glorify that moment, but My heavenly Father said: 'This is My beloved Son, in Whom I am well pleased; hear Him.' Then I told My apostles that Elijah will come before I return, but that the spirit of Elijah had already come in St. John the Baptist. St. John taught the people to repent and prepare for the Lamb of God to come. Then he pointed Me out as the Lamb, and the Promised Messiah, who would redeem mankind. You have St. John already announcing My coming in the womb of St. Elizabeth when he stirred to acknowledge My Presence when My Blessed Mother came to help St. Elizabeth. Now in Advent, you will be reading St. John's account of how he prepared the way of My coming. When I return, you will see the two prophets Elijah and Enoch, who will prepare My way again. Rejoice as you celebrate My coming feast of Christmas. You have yet to rejoice again when I will come in victory over the Antichrist and Satan, when I will make all things new in My Era of Peace."*

Later, at our house with the Adoration DVD, I could see one snowstorm after another. Jesus said: *"My people, now your weather forecasters are naming the snowstorms, and you are up to your fifth storm. Your snow levels are a bit over normal already, and you have not even turned to winter on December 21st. Deep cold and plenty of snow are already the signature of this year's winter. Many people in the North have been suffering from heavy snows, and some have had ice storms with freezing rain. Pray for all the people who are suffering hardships as a result of your severe weather. The one good thing that comes from these storms, is that neighbors are helping each other with the plowing, and sharing food and heat with those who lost their power. You all know how hard it is to be without heat, food, or water. Again, I remind you to share your donations with your food shelves, and pray for the poor that they will find what they need to survive."*

Sunday, December 15, 2013: (3rd Sunday of Advent)

At Holy Name after Holy Communion, I could see a small stream of fresh water. Jesus said: *"My people, today you are celebrating Gaudete or Joy Sunday of Advent when the vestments are in pink. I am showing you a stream of water that represents the Living Water that I give you in Holy Communion. This is My living Presence when I am with you intimately in your soul. You can rejoice every time that you receive Me at Mass. You are preparing to meet Me at Christmas with your gift of love both for Me and your neighbors. Sharing gifts with friends and family is a happy time of the year, and you see family members that live far away from you. You can travel quite fast in your cars and planes in good weather. It was more difficult for My parents to travel on foot from Nazareth to Bethlehem for the census. Your travel can also help you in evangelizing souls in various cities. Keep struggling to share My Word with all the nations, so they can experience My love and My sacraments."*

Monday, December 16, 2013:

At St. John the Evangelist after Holy Communion, I could see people having trouble driving and moving the snow. Jesus said: *"My people, in the winter you may have to deal with annoyances from ice and snow on your windshields. When it is cold, the ice builds up on your windshield blades, and the salt mist blinds your vision. Even when you have these problems, do not let these things disturb your peace. Take some time to clean the ice off the wheel wells and your windshield blades, and continue on without getting upset. It can even be unsafe for your travel, without proper vision for driving. Have patience also with slow drivers, where there is a lot of snow on the road. At times it may be better not to travel during snow blizzards, if you can avoid it. Being kind and understanding of your fellow motorists, will cause less accidents, and not cause you to get angry over the little things. By keeping peace in your soul, you can be more loving of your neighbors."*

Later, at St. Joseph's Place after Holy Communion, I could see a coming of Jesus at the end of a tunnel, when people were faced with their mini-judgment. Jesus said: *"My people, many of you are waiting to celebrate My birthday on Christmas. The vision was showing you another coming, when you will come to Me in a tunnel outside of time, and outside of your body. This will be the illumination of your conscience, or some call it the Warning. This will truly be a wake-up call for all souls to see how I will judge them up to this one point in their lives. You will have no excuses, because you will be reviewing your actual words and actions, which you will not be able to deny as the truth. You will see where your soul is headed, when I give you your mini-judgment. You will have a second chance to improve your spiritual lives, if you change your life for the better. Prepare your soul with frequent Confession, and you could avoid any judgment to hell.*

Be thankful that I will give every sinner a chance to be saved. I am a gracious and loving God, and I will give a heavenly reward to any repentant sinner."

Tuesday, December 17, 2013:

At Holy Name after Holy Communion, I could see the wall of a dam holding back the flood waters. Jesus said: *"My people, as you can see in the genealogy of My family, there were all kinds of people including those who were worse sinners than the rest. In reading these names, there are stories about each of them, and you are seeing all the human weaknesses in their sins. I love all of My creations, even though they have committed great sins of lust and murder. The important part of life is to not only accept that you are a sinner, but that you need to repent of your sins in Confession. Without the forgiveness of your sins when*

you come to Me, you cannot enter heaven. When you come to Me, I will forgive the worst sinner, and restore My graces in your souls. Do not let pride make you think that you are not sinning. Man is imperfect from Adam's sin, yet I love all sinners enough to die for their redemption. This is why My faithful need to come to Confession at least monthly, so you can have your soul pure whenever I will call you home in death. Guard your souls from sin, and use My sacraments to keep holy."

Later, at St. Theodore's Adoration, I could see a large pile of pearls, gold, and silver in a vault. Jesus said: *"My people, as you hear people buying tickets for $600 million sweepstakes, you can see their desire to strike it rich. Others love their rich homes and expensive cars. You have a society in America that is in love with riches and possessions. When money and possessions become a god for people, they are worshiping these things instead of Me. These are the same people who are also in love with their sexual pleasures. All of these sins breed more evil in your society. It is hard to find My faithful prayer warriors among the many sinners in your country. I keep mentioning how there is not enough prayer being said to offset all of your sins. Your society also has the blood of many abortions on its hands. As your disasters increase, you will be approaching the end days when My faithful will need to seek My refuges to avoid the Antichrist. I will bring your country to its knees when martial law will allow the one world people to take over your country. Trust in My protection from the evil ones, before I will bring My victory over all the evil of this world. Your reward will be in My Era of Peace, and later in heaven."*

Wednesday, December 18, 2013:

At St. John the Evangelist after Holy Communion, I could see people setting out the silverware and plates for a Christmas dinner. Jesus said: *"My people, many of you are making preparations for Christmas by baking cookies and putting up your decorations. You are finishing up your Christmas gift buying, and you have sent out your Christmas cards, for those who send cards. Making preparations to receive your family from out of town, is another labor of love. You also need to buy enough food for the family staying over. All of these preparations take time and some money, but it is a joyful season to share your love with your family members. Many in the North will have a white Christmas with some melting of the snow. Pray for good weather for those who have to travel any distance. It is always a joy to share your gifts, and to share your meals with each other. The Magi shared their gifts with Me, and I share Myself with you at every Mass to nourish your spiritual life. I rejoice to see all of your families getting together. Give them a good example by coming to church for Christmas. Remember to try and get to Confession before Christmas. I love all of you, and I pray that you can share your love with Me in return."*

Later, at St. Joseph's Place after Holy Communion, I could see a long table that was ready for a wedding feast on earth. Then I saw a more glorious banquet place set up for a wedding feast in heaven. Jesus said: *"My people, you have heard Me speak of the Wedding feast at*

Thursday, December 19, 2013:

At Holy Name after Holy Communion, I could see the focus on the miracle and gift of new life in babies that are born. Jesus said: *"My people, today, in the Scriptures there is a focus on miracle births, by man's standard. Both Samson and St. John the Baptist were miracle births to older barren women that were announced by an angel. For Me all things are possible, beyond the natural order of births. Even My own birth was more miraculous. Again, My birth was announced by St. Gabriel the Archangel. I was conceived by the Holy Spirit in a sinless virgin of My Blessed Mother. Even births by the normal course are miracles of life, in how they are formed in the womb. I place a soul in each baby at conception, and I give each of you a guardian angel to watch over you. You should be joyful to accept every birth, even those who are born outside of wedlock. I have given you an example of normal married life from Adam and Eve. Such relations should only occur under the bond of marriage. This is living according to My Commandments, and children should be brought up in an environment of married love. Even though many are living together, it is still sinful to be fornicating without marriage. Encourage your children to get married before having any children. This is the way of heaven, and not the way of human lust."*

Later, at the Eternal Father prayer group at Holy Name Adoration, I could see the readings from the daily Masses getting closer to Jesus' birth. Jesus said: *"My people, in your readings you are hearing the accounts about St. Joseph, St. Elizabeth, St. John the Baptist, and My own Blessed Mother. Every year you celebrate My birthday on Christmas, and you are all joyful in this season of love and sharing gifts. Overlook all the shopping for gifts, and focus more on My Incarnation as a man, so I could offer My life up for mankind's sins. You all love celebrating the birth of a baby, especially the birth of your Savior. Rejoice with the shepherds, the angels, and the Magi, who came to give glory to God in Me."*

I could see how our government is trying to control our lives in telling us what light bulbs to buy and what health insurance to buy. Jesus said: *"My people, you are seeing how the government is slowly taking over many parts of your life by fiat rule. You are seeing regulations soon that will outlaw incandescent light bulbs starting on January 1st when 40 and 60 watt bulbs will not be made any more. You also are being forced to buy health insurance that pays for more health coverage than you need."*

I could see more discontent with Obamacare as people are still trying to find out the cost of their new health insurance. Jesus said: *"My people, many people have had trouble in signing up for Obamacare because of the non-working website. Once people are signed up, then they need to contact the insurance companies to begin paying their premiums. This connection to insurance companies has yet to be put on the website. It is still a problem to find out the actual cost of a person's insurance premiums. The government is trying to put this knowledge of the premiums off until after the 2014 elections. Once the people realize how much their full health insurance premiums will cost, then they will be outraged at the high costs and the high deductibles. Those, who were dropped, are now paying much higher premiums. This law will be so disliked by the paying middle class, that the Democrats could lose some elections. It is those, who do not have to pay, that are in favor of this transfer of wealth. Many people will also find difficulty in getting a doctor. Pray for a fair resolution of this problem of Obamacare."*

I could see a temporary calm in Congress over the budget. Jesus said: *"My people, your partisan politics have made an attempt to settle your budget debate. Unfortunately, this is a short peace, as the next storms will be coming with a raising of the debt ceiling, and immigration reform. When you have divided government, it is hard to get bills passed that both sides will favor. Keep praying for your Congress people so they can agree on what is good for your people."*

I could see a thaw melting the snow, but then more ice storms are being forecasted. Jesus said: *"My people, when you have freezing rain, you can have ice build up on the trees that can snap tree limbs and bring down power lines. Be prepared for more power outages when these ice storms will come into the Northeast. These disasters will continue throughout this winter season because of your sins."*

I could see people praying the octave prayers before Christmas for the baby Jesus celebration. Jesus said: *"My people, there are certain Spanish groups who are faithful in their prayers to the Infant Jesus. There is a great need for prayer in your world because of the many sins. Along with your prayers, you could help the poor with your donations for their food and shelter. You share gifts with your friends, and you expect something in return. When you give to the poor, you do not expect anything in return, but you will store up treasure in heaven for your charity."*

I could see people sharing a Christmas dinner. I could also see many poor people in need of a meal. Jesus said: *"My people, you can share your donations of food and money with your local food shelves. You can also give your time to help bring some food to those who are in need at your soup kitchens. There is joy in your heart when you can feed the hungry by bringing food to their houses, or by feeding them hot meals as for the homeless. You can also make some donations toward helping people to find shelter or donating to help the poor pay their heating bills. The Christmas spirit of sharing comes right from the love in your hearts."*

Friday, December 20, 2013;

At St. John the Evangelist after Holy Communion, I could see the beauty of the Incarnation of God the Son into a man. Jesus said: *"My people, in today's Gospel, you see My Blessed Mother accepting the angel's request to be My mother. It is hard for man to understand how condescending it is for Me as God the Son, to be incarnated as a man. This is a mystery which I performed, so I could see and experience all of your human discomforts. It also was the will of God the Father for Me to become a man because the prophets foretold that a Redeemer would be sent to bring salvation to mankind because of your sins. Once I was incarnated as a human, I could now sacrifice My life in atonement for all of your sins. Now heaven would be open to those sinners who were baptized, and repented of their sins. I am happy to forgive your sins, and restore My grace to your soul. Rejoice in My Incarnation, that made your salvation possible."*

Later, at St. Theodore's tabernacle, I could see a plane on the ground, and it had caught on fire. Jesus said: *"My people, during the winter, you have had many flights cancelled when you have heavy snowstorms. Now, you are having rain on the snow, and you are seeing considerable fog. During the winter, your planes have to have de-icing fluid sprayed on the wings to avoid ice building up on the cold surfaces. The plane on fire in the vision, could come from many causes, and especially from weather-related problems. Whenever you take a flight in the winter, you need to pray for good weather, and your St. Michael's prayer as you do for your car. Praying for safe travel, puts yourself in My hands, and your guardian angel's care. You have seen many delays with your plane flights, but you want to be in a well running plane, and not one with bad instruments. You can also pray for all the other flights, so they will go well without any accidents."*

Saturday, December 21, 2013: (St. Peter Canisius)

At the Sisters of St. Joseph mother house after Holy Communion, I could see a live living tunnel like the inside of a large fish. Jesus said: *"My people, when you come to My Light in the Warning, you will travel through a live living tunnel outside of your body and outside of time. You are preparing to celebrate when I was born years ago in a stable in Bethlehem. I came as a man so I could suffer for your sins and redeem your souls. You will see Me again in My Warning, as I will have mercy on all souls. They will have a second chance to improve their lives, so they will be directed to heaven. At the end of the tribulation, you will see My coming in victory over the evil ones when I will separate those going to hell from My faithful who will be saved in heaven. This tribulation will be your living purgatory on earth. Prepare for My coming again by frequent Confession of at least once a month. Those, who struggle to be obedient to My Commandments, and are sorry for their sins, will be saved in heaven."*

Later, at Holy Name Nocturnal Hour, I could see the bread and wine consecrated at a Mass into the Body and Blood of Jesus. Jesus said: *"My people, I have talked to you many times about My Real Presence in My consecrated Host. This Eucharistic mystery of My Real Presence is hard for man to understand, but it can only be accepted in faith. I can do all things, even the impossible. So if I want to allow the priest to consecrate the bread and wine into My Body and Blood, I can do it. Whether people want to believe it or not, I am still present, just the same. Those who have weak faith, cannot or have difficulty in accepting My Real Presence in My Host. If you truly believe in My Real Presence, then you will have great joy every time that you receive Me in Holy Communion. Only My true believers genuflect to My tabernacle, and come to visit Me in Adoration in My monstrance or in My tabernacle. Those who do not believe in My Real Presence, have little reverence for My Host, and rarely visit My tabernacle because they do not believe that I am there. Encourage people to believe in My Real Presence because this is the gift of My very Self to you in My Blessed Sacrament."*

Sunday, December 22, 2013: (4th Sunday of Advent)

At Holy Name after Holy Communion, I could see the rough terrain that St. Joseph and the Blessed Mother had to travel to Bethlehem from Nazareth. Jesus said: *"My people, because of the Roman census, My parents had to travel to Bethlehem because they were both from the lineage of King David. In My day you had to travel on foot or use a donkey to carry people and their belongings. You have traveled to Israel, and you know how rough and hilly the roads are. Some traveled in caravans for safety from the thieves. You remember this when I was lost in the temple because My parents were in a caravan. Today, you can travel in airplanes or cars, so your travel time is shorter for longer distances. Many families can come together for Christmas because of your shorter travel times. It is your weather conditions that could slow down your travel with snow or freezing rain. You had some freezing rain on your trees, but it was not severe, and it will melt with a warm day. Have a little understanding then, for how much My parents had to endure in their travel, and how difficult it was to find a place to stay. The cave with the animals was not the best place for Me to be born, but it was a humbling experience."*

Monday, December 23, 2013:

At St. John the Evangelist after Holy Communion, I could see the prophets of old and the prophets of today. Jesus said: *"My people, in the Old Testament readings, it speaks of Elijah coming before My coming to earth. Indeed, you have the spirit of Elijah coming in St. John the Baptist as My herald in the desert. It is appropriate to celebrate St. John the Baptist's birth before My birth. Later, he called the people to repent and be baptized. He prepared the way of My coming, and even baptized Me in the Jordan River. In every age I call up My prophets to prepare for My coming again. Even today, there are many prophets speaking of the coming tribulation of the Antichrist. You, My son, are one of them who go forth preparing the people by encouraging them to come to Confession to avoid any judgment to hell in the Warning. After the time of the Antichrist, I will come to separate the evil ones into hell, and My faithful will come into My Era of Peace, and later into heaven. Rejoice not only in celebrating Christmas, but you will rejoice further in My victory over the evil ones."*

Tuesday, December 24, 2013: (Midnight Mass)

At St. John the Evangelist after Holy Communion, I could see the glory of the angels singing about the coming of Jesus to the shepherds. Jesus said: *"My people, in today's reading, you heard of how St. Joseph and My Blessed Mother had to travel from Nazareth to Bethlehem because of the Roman census. This was most difficult for My Blessed Mother because she was forced to travel while she was pregnant with Me. They went through even more trouble to find a secluded place in a stable where she could give birth to Me. In the vision you saw the angels singing to the shepherds, who were led to give praise and honor to Me as an infant. Many people celebrate Christmas by sharing gifts, but I am the Gift to mankind because I came to offer My life for your sins. I ask all of you to bring your prayers and earthly sufferings to Me as your gift. Rejoice in the glory of My coming at Christmas."*

Wednesday, December 25, 2013: (Christmas Day)

At Holy Name after Holy Communion, I could see Jesus come to us in the Eucharist. Jesus said: *"My people, today you celebrate My birth over two thousand years ago, when I was born in a manger in Bethlehem. Many did not realize the significance of My Incarnation as a man, but My parents knew because of the angels who told them. The angels sang praise to Me, and they encouraged the shepherds to visit My crib. I was born in humble surroundings, but truly I am your King. I was sent by My heavenly Father to do His Will, which eventually led to My giving up of My life for everyone's sins, and the salvation of mankind. Sing your praises of My coming, because through Me, you are saved. You can only come to heaven through Me. All of heaven rejoiced with the angels, as they celebrated the arrival of man's Redeemer. I love all of you so much that I came to earth as a man, so I could die as a Lamb for all of your sins. Rejoice with Me at every Mass, when I come to you in Holy Communion."*

Thursday, December 26, 2013: (St. Stephen)

At Holy Name after Holy Communion, I could see St. Stephen being stoned to death, and he forgave his persecutors as Jesus did on the cross. Jesus said: *"My people, proclaiming My Gospel Word of love and obedience to My Commandments, will not be easy in front of your politically correct society. Your society makes killing My babies in the womb legal in your courts. Your courts and states are now making same-sex marriage legal as a right. Living together in fornication is also accepted by your society. These things are all mortal sins in My eyes, and they should be avoided to save your souls. You have Confession to confess these sins, but for people to defend these actions as acceptable and legal, shows you how depraved your society is. It is not easy to live out your Christian faith in public, because to stand up against these sins of abortion, fornication, and homosexual acts, you will be persecuted for My Name's sake. People, who are committing these sins, do not want to be criticized for doing something wrong, because the evil ones control your media, and they will persecute anyone who goes against them. It is the evil ones who are dictating what is politically correct, and the one world people are led by Satan to advocate these sins. Even if you are persecuted in public, it is still a Christian's duty to advise your brother when he is committing serious sin as abortion, fornication, or homosexual acts. Those, who are willing to stand up for their religious beliefs, will have their reward in heaven, even if you have to die as a martyr for your faith."*

Later, at the Eternal Father prayer group at Holy Name Adoration, I could see families still sharing with themselves for Christmas. Jesus said: *"My people, I want you to think of all the gifts that have been given to you, and how you should thank Me for everything. I give you Myself as your gift in My Blessed Sacrament. For all of your families, you have gifts in your spouse, your children, and your grandchildren. Coming together as family is special at Christmas. You have gifts of jobs, homes, and your possessions to survive. I see to all of your needs, so thank Me for all that you have."*

I could see some people who are suffering sicknesses, and others who are well. Jesus said: *"My people, you cannot be sure that you will be here tomorrow. Your health is another important gift, because many are suffering from bad knees, bad legs, diabetes, high blood pressure, and many other chronic conditions. Pray for the grace to suffer through any health problems, and be willing to visit the sick and console the dying."*

I could see some people who were suffering with power outages from the recent ice storm. Jesus said: *"My people, you are seeing people in Canada and other parts of America who are dealing with ice on the trees and no electricity. You remember well how it was a struggle to keep your house warm, and provide food and water in the cold of winter during an ice storm. Pray for all of these people that they could have their power restored. Again, be thankful if you have power and heat during the winter."*

I could see people praying in a prayer group. Jesus said: *"My people, I am pleased with your prayers because they are multiplied in your prayer group. I want you to encourage your people to pray daily, because there are not enough people praying, and I rely on My prayer warriors to make up for all of those people who are not praying. You pray your three rosaries and your Divine Mercy Chaplet as a minimum for the day. Do not forget to pray them, and make them up the next day if you are not able to complete them. The sins in the world are great, and it is only through prayer that they can be atoned."*

I could see many Christians who are being persecuted and even martyred for their faith. Jesus said: *"My people, just as I had to suffer persecution, so My faithful will also suffer at the hands of the worldly people. Some Christians are being martyred as St. Stephen was, and many are being persecuted because of their holy witness to the world. Do not worry about being politically correct, but speak about your faith in public, so you are a good Christian example to your family and others."*

I could see people sharing gifts with the poor. Jesus said: *"My people, you have shared your gifts with one another, but you should leave room in your heart to share prayers and donations to the poor. If you could spend so much on all of your Christmas gifts, you could spend a little to help the poor. When you help the poor, you are helping Me in them because you are all a part of My human family. Have compassion on them in providing food and shelter, and you will be storing up treasure in heaven for your judgment."*

I could see people living their lives without realizing that life is God's gift to us, and we should treasure it as precious. Jesus said: *"My people, life and your soul is one of your greatest gifts to be alive and experience*

My love for you. This is why you should be doing all that you can to stop abortions and encourage these mothers to have their babies. I love My little ones, and I do not want to see you killing My babies in abortion. Do not deny these little ones the chance to experience life as you have had it. Do not accept the death culture's word, but do what you can to protest abortions at the abortion clinics, and your marches in Washington, D.C. on January 22, the anniversary of Row vs. Wade decision that supports abortion."

Friday, December 27, 2013: (St. John the Evangelist)

At St. John the Evangelist after Holy Communion, I could see a flashback to Ephesus, where St. John was buried. St. John said: *"My son, you remember well the words that I gave you when you came to my burial place in Ephesus, Turkey. The Lord showed me many visions of the end times, and what it would be like during the tribulation of the Antichrist. He also showed me His victory over the evil ones, even as He showed me the empty tomb in His victory over sin and death. I loved Jesus so much, and I was blessed to take care of His Blessed Mother. When I gave you a message at Ephesus, I wanted you to continue on with my mission of preparing the people for the end times. The Lord has shared many details about how He will be protecting His people at His refuges. Even though refuges were not explicitly stated in the Gospels, there were accounts of Elijah hiding in the cave, and even the stable of Jesus' birth looked like a cave of protection. I rejoiced to see Jesus appear to us after His Resurrection, and on Mt. Tabor in His Transfiguration. You have a deep faith and trust in My beloved Jesus. Keep Him at the center of your life, and He will be with you to complete your mission."*

Later, at St. Theodore's tabernacle, I could see a dark bedroom scene with a bed, as this was a source of sin for many people that are fornicating as unmarried people. Jesus said: *"My people, the problem with your world is the rampant sexual sins, and the abortions that are killing My babies. I have told you before that not enough people are praying to atone for all of these sins. So pray to Me to double and multiply your prayers for the sin of the world. Many of your people also are worshiping money, possessions, and sports more than Me. Much of this sin will not change until I bring My Warning, when all sinners will have a chance to convert their lives. Until this happens, I want you to encourage the people to pray more, go to Confession more frequently, and make visits to My tabernacle in Adoration. By your example, you can help people to lead a good Christian life in following My Commandments. Once the Warning comes, the people will be so shaken by their sinful lives, that they will desire forgiveness of their sins in Confession. It will be at that time that those, who are away from Me, will be more open to your evangelization efforts. All the prayers that you have been praying for your family and friends will be most honored in their lifestyle conversions. More sinners will be saved, but still some will love their sins more than Me. In the end, it will be the people's free will decision to accept Me, that will determine their soul's destination either to heaven or hell."*

Saturday, December 28, 2013: (Holy Innocents)
At Sacred Heart Cathedral after Holy Communion, I could see the Roman soldiers killing the babies with their swords in Bethlehem. Jesus said: *"My people, St. Joseph was warned by an angel in a dream to take Me and My Blessed Mother to Egypt so Herod could not kill Me. I stayed there until Herod died, and My family returned to Nazareth. These Holy Innocents were defenseless against the brutality of Herod's soldiers, who were ordered to kill all the infants up to two years of age. Today, in your abortion clinics you are seeing the same brutality of the doctors who crush the heads of*

the babies, and evacuate their little bodies from the womb. Abortion is one of the worst crimes that you could commit because I am in charge of who is born and when you die. When you kill these innocent and defenseless babies, you are denying My plan for each life that is taken. Once there is a conception, a soul is placed in that fertilized egg, and a guardian angel is assigned to that new life. When you abort a baby, the guardian angel of that life returns to heaven to give witness that a life has been aborted. It is these sins of abortion that weigh heavily against a nation that has laws or decisions that allow such killing. Woe to America for allowing and even advocating such crimes. Your country will pay dearly for the blood on your hands. Please pray for the stoppage of abortion and publicly protest this injustice. If you do nothing about this killing of babies, then your inaction will be condoning these crimes of murder."*

Later, at St. Theodore's tabernacle I could see an infant king being carried in a luxurious coach with true royalty as a king. Jesus said: *"My people, I had a choice of how I would come and present Myself to the world. I could have come as royalty in a coach with much power and control, but I chose to come as a humble infant in a stable. I chose to focus on delivering My Gospel words of love, and proclaim that the Kingdom of God is at hand. I have power over the demons and the universe, which is why I cast out demons, healed people, and even calmed the storms at sea. I did not come to be served, but I came to serve sinners. I eventually, died to atone for your sins, and I offer everyone an opportunity to be saved in heaven. I do not force My love on you, but I desire you to love Me of your own free will. You have a choice of being with the love of your Savior forever, or you can be with the anger of the devil in the flames of hell where he hates you. Your soul will exist for all eternity, so choose your destination by your actions. If you love Me and desire heaven, then you will give yourself over to My Will, so you can do everything out of love for Me. I will see the sincerity of the intentions in your heart to know that you truly love Me. Reach out to your neighbors to bring them closer to Me, so they can be converted. My desire is to save all souls from hell."*

Sunday, December 29, 2013: (Holy Family Sunday)

At Holy Name after Holy Communion I could see the Holy Family together in Bethlehem. Jesus said: *"My people, this day you honor My Holy Family, and you should see us as a model for all family households. The children should be brought up in an environment of love with a loving mother and a loving father. When you have divorce and co-habitation, the children are either missing a parent, or their parents are living in sin as a bad example. Even married couples need to avoid birth control, because every marriage act needs to be open to having children. Family planning of using infertile times, is allowed. When your society treats life as precious, then you would not have abortions. Families need to patch up any disagreements, so you do not live with endless grudges. Life is too short to not live in love of each other. When spouses work at good communications and love, then there will be less divorces. When the family comes to Sunday Mass, monthly Confession, and prays daily, then you are inviting Me to be a part of your family. Your Lord should be the most loved in all the world. When you pray every day, you are telling Me how much you love Me. The family should be the basic units of your society. The devil is constantly trying to break up families, especially through communism and socialism. Follow My ways instead of the ways of the world, and your families will be thriving in My love."*

Monday, December 30, 2013: (Mary Buechel Funeral Mass)

At St. Charles Borromeo Church after Holy Communion I could see Mary at a prayer group. Mary said: *"I am happy to see all of my family and friends who came to my funeral Mass. I thank everyone for helping me in my later years. I love all of you. As you heard from Father, I was always filled with the joy of the Holy Spirit. You know about our prayer group when we spoke in tongues. I also was happy in sharing our presentation on Garabandal, Spain. You are familiar with many of the words on the Warning and the Great Chastisement. I am in heaven already, and my relatives and Bill were there to greet me when I came. I was blessed to die on Christmas, when Our Blessed Mother takes souls to heaven. I will be praying for all of My family and friends, so you can be with me in heaven one day."*

Later, at St. Theodore's tabernacle I could see a casket and a focus on an AK-15 gun and a bomb. Jesus said: *"My people, this casket is a representation of how many people died from terrorist activities this year, either from AK-15 guns or bombs. This same kind of behavior will occur next year as well, because the one world people thrive on instilling fear in the people. Continuous terrorist attacks are one of the three means for initiating a national martial law. The other two are a crash of your financial system, and a pandemic virus in the chemtrails. Perpetrating these activities would be how the one world people plan to cause a takeover of America through martial law. During martial law the army or mercenary forces, will illegally takeover your government and your local police forces. This will be a dictatorial running of your country by the executive authority of the acting President through Executive Orders. This authority will be invoked by the acting President who will declare a state of martial law. He will have control over food, transportation, and the running of your country. Once such a martial law is invoked, the authorities will be eliminating all of those people who do not go along with the new world order, and those who do not take the chip in the body. This will be the time when My faithful will be called to come to My refuges for protection. These events will lead quickly into the declaration of the Antichrist in a world takeover. Your acting President will be replaced by the Antichrist's leaders. Fear not these evil ones because the reign of the Antichrist will be brief, when I will bring My victory over all the evil ones. My faithful will see their reward in My Era of Peace, and later in heaven."*

Tuesday, December 31, 2013: (Vigil of the Solemnity of Mary)
At Holy Name after Holy Communion I could see Mary, and Jesus was in the manger. Jesus said: *"My people, My Blessed Mother had her greatest moment in giving birth to Me in Bethlehem. She also had an important moment in saying 'yes' to the Archangel Gabriel when she affirmed that she would be My mother. I had prepared her for that moment for many years, even when she was conceived without sin. The shepherds and the angels gave praise to Me as her Son. My Incarnation as a man is the beginning of man's salvation, once I was on the earth. My birth was quickly followed by persecution as Herod wanted to kill Me. An angel guided St. Joseph to take the Holy Family to Egypt, to protect My life from Herod, who killed the Holy Innocents of Bethlehem. Rejoice in My Blessed Mother's role of the Nativity Scene because she had to endure the hard travel. She is watching over all of*

you with her mantle of protection."

Later, at our home we were watching the Adoration DVD and I could keep seeing major disasters all over the world. Jesus said: *"My people, you will continue to see many weather related disasters, and some of them will be caused by the HAARP machine. The one world people know how much damage this microwave machine can cause with your weather and earthquakes. They will try to blame it on Me, but they know the real cause. This is part of their plan to ruin your economy with one disaster after another, so they can precipitate a martial law. If martial law is declared, or chips in the body are mandated, these will be the events that will cause you to come to My refuges of protection. Have your things packed, so you can leave for My refuges on short notice. Those, who leave on time, will be protected. Those, who take too long to leave, could risk being captured by the men in black. This is why some will be martyred for their faith, while others will be safe at My refuges. Those, who are not prepared, may suffer the most for not listening to My words of warning."*

Index

Obamacare (Jesus)	10/1/2013	priests (Jesus)	11/20/2013
Obamacare (Jesus)	11/13/2013	priests & bishops (Jesus)	11/18/2013
Obamacare (Jesus)	12/19/2013	prophets of end days (Jesus)	12/23/2013
Obamacare (Jesus)	11/7/2013	pure soul (Jesus)	10/24/2013
Obamacare (Jesus)	12/5/2013	purgatory (Jesus)	11/2/2013
Obamacare internet (Jesus)	10/10/2013	purgatory, souls in (Jesus)	10/31/2013
Obamacare taxes (Jesus)	10/31/2013	Real Presence in Host (Jesus)	12/21/2013
Obamacare waivers (Jesus)	10/24/2013	Redeemer as covenant (Jesus)	10/24/2013
obedience to God (Jesus)	11/6/2013	refuge builders (Jesus)	10/25/2013
one world people (Jesus)	10/15/2013	refuge farming (Jesus)	10/11/2013
one world people (Jesus)	10/5/2013	refuge fuels (Jesus)	12/11/2013
pain offered up (Jesus)	10/30/2013	refuge life (Jesus)	10/3/2013
pain, ailments (Jesus)	11/7/2013	refuge meat (Jesus)	10/31/2013
peace in soul (Jesus)	10/24/2013	refuge needs provided (Jesus)	12/11/2013
penance for Confession (Jesus)	11/22/2013	refuge of sinners (Mary)	12/12/2013
persecution (Jesus)	11/18/2013	refuge ovens (Jesus)	11/5/2013
personal message (Jesus)	11/27/2013	refuge sign, train (Jesus)	10/25/2013
personal message (Jesus)	11/30/2013	refuge time (Jesus)	11/17/2013
Philippine rescue effort (Jesus)	11/14/2013	renewed earth (Jesus)	12/10/2013
Philippine typhoon (Jesus)	11/7/2013	Reparation Mass (Jesus)	10/21/2013
pictures of family (Jesus)	12/8/2013	Reparation Masses (Jesus)	11/23/2013
poor donations (Jesus)	12/13/2013	repent now (Jesus)	11/30/2013
power outages (Jesus)	12/9/2013	Right to Life (Jesus)	10/24/2013
power outages (Jesus)	11/7/2013	Rock of St. Peter (Jesus)	12/5/2013
power outages (Jesus)	11/1/2013	rosary, scapular (Mary)	11/12/2013
power outages (Jesus)	12/26/2013	Sacred Heart enthronement (Jesus)	11/21/2013
praises to (Jesus) (Jesus)	12/25/2013	sainthood (Jesus)	12/7/2013
pray from the heart (Jesus)	10/26/2013	sainthood goal (Jesus)	11/1/2013
prayer groups (Jesus)	10/10/2013	saints (Jesus)	11/1/2013
prayer intentions (Jesus)	10/27/2013	Salvatore Matano (Jesus)	11/11/2013
prayer needed (Mary)	10/7/2013	same sex marriage,euthanasia (Jesus)	
prayer time needed (Jesus)	10/26/2013		10/3/2013
prayer types (Jesus)	10/20/2013	save souls (Jesus)	11/17/2013
prayer warriors (Jesus)	12/26/2013	schismatic church (Jesus)	10/12/2013
prayer warriors (Jesus)	10/10/2013	schismatic church (Jesus)	11/18/2013
prayers (Jesus)	10/9/2013	serpent as evil one (Jesus)	10/10/2013
prayers for sinners (Jesus)	10/10/2013	serving God (Jesus)	11/12/2013
prayers from the heart (Jesus)	12/3/2013	sexual sins, abortions (Jesus)	12/27/2013
priest intentions (Jesus)	12/3/2013	shadow government (Jesus)	10/15/2013

More Messages

If you would like to take advantage of more precious words from Jesus and Mary and apply them to your lives, read the first three volumes of messages and visions given to us through John's special gift. Each book contains a full year of daily messages and visions. As Jesus and Mary said in volume IV:

Listen to My words of warning, and you will be ready to share in the beauty of the Second Coming. Jesus 7/4/96

I will work miracles of conversion on those who read these books with an open mind. Jesus 9/5/96

Prepare for the Great Tribulation and the Era of Peace

Volume I - *July 1993 to June 1994,*
ISBN# 1-882972-69-4, 256pp. $7.95

Volume II - *July 1994 to June 1995,*
ISBN# 1-882972-72-4, 352pp. $8.95

Volume III - *July 1995 to July 10, 1996,*
ISBN# 1-882972-77-5, 384pp. $8.95

Volume IV - *July 11, 1996 to Sept. 30, 1996,*
ISBN# 1-882972-91-0, 104pp. $3.95

Volume V - *Oct. 1, 1996 to Dec. 31, 1996,*
ISBN# 1-882972-97-X, 120pp. $3.95

Volume VI - *Jan. 1, 1997 to Mar. 31, 1997,*
ISBN# 1-57918-002-7, 112pp. $3.95

Volume VII - *April 1, 1997 to June 30, 1997,*
ISBN# 1-57918-010-8, 112pp. $3.95

Volume VIII - *July 1, 1997 to Sept. 30, 1997,*
ISBN# 1-57918-053-1, 128pp. $3.95

Volume IX - *Oct. 1, 1997 to Dec. 31, 1997,*
ISBN# 1-57918-066-3, 168pp. $3.95

Volume X - *Jan. 1, 1998 to Mar. 31, 1998,*
ISBN# 1-57918-073-6, 116pp. $3.95

Volume XI - *Apr. 1, 1998 to June 30, 1998,*
ISBN# 1-57918-096-5, 128pp. $3.95

Volume XII - *July 1, 1998 to Sept. 30, 1998,*
ISBN# 1-57918-105-8, 128pp. $3.95

Volume XIII - *Oct. 1, 1998 to Dec. 31, 1998,*
ISBN# 1-57918-113-9, 134pp. $3.95

Volume XIV - *Jan. 1, 1999 to Mar. 31, 1999,*
ISBN# 1-57918-115-5, 128pp. $3.95

Volume XV - *Apr. 1, 1999 to June 30, 1999,*
ISBN# 1-57918-122-8, 128pp. $3.95

Volume XVI - *July 1, 1999 to Sept. 31, 1999,*
ISBN# 1-57918-126-0, 136pp. $3.95

Volume XVII - *Oct. 1, 1999 to Dec. 31, 1999,*
ISBN# 1-57918-156-2, 136pp. $3.95

Volume XVII - *Jan. 1, 2000 to Mar. 31, 2000,*
ISBN# 1-57918-158-9, 136pp. $3.95

Volume XIX - *Apr. 1, 2000 to June 30, 2000,*
ISBN# 1-57918-160-0, 136pp. $3.95

Volume XX - *July 1, 2000 to Sept. 30, 2000,*
ISBN# 1-57918-162-7, 136pp. $3.95

Volume XXI - *Oct. 1, 2000 to Dec. 31, 2000,*
ISBN# 1-57918-160-0, 136pp. $3.95

Volume XXII - *Jan. 1, 2001 to Mar. 31, 2001,*
ISBN# 1-57918-172-4, 136pp. $3.95

Volume XXIII - *Apr. 1, 2001 to June 30, 2001,*
ISBN# 1-57918-173-2, 136pp. $3.95

Volume XXIV - *July 1, 2001 to Sept. 30, 2001,*
ISBN# 1-57918-174-0, 136pp. $3.95